THE YEAR AMERICA DIED

GREG JOHNSON

Counter-Currents Publishing Ltd.
San Francisco
2021

Copyright © 2021 by Greg Johnson
All rights reserved

Cover image:
January 6, 2021 Protests, Washington, D.C.

Cover design by Kevin I. Slaughter

Published in the United States by
COUNTER-CURRENTS PUBLISHING LTD.
P.O. Box 22638
San Francisco, CA 94122
USA
http://www.counter-currents.com/

Hardcover ISBN: 978-1-64264-171-4
Paperback ISBN: 978-1-64264-172-1
E-book ISBN: 978-1-64264-173-8

Contents

1. The Year America Died ❖ 1

The Globalvirus
2. How COVID-19 Will Change the World ❖ 5
3. I'm Changing My Tune About COVID-19 ❖ 13

The Race War
4. Black Lies Matter ❖ 18
5. Do Black Lives Matter? ❖ 23
6. George Floyd Got Justice ❖ 31
7. Verdict on America ❖ 35
8. Amnesty Your Ancestors ❖ 39

The Trumpocalypse
9. The 2018 Midterm Elections: A Near Death Experience? ❖ 42
10. Why White Nationalists Like Andrew Yang ❖ 46
11. The Iran Opportunity ❖ 56
12. Wignats Whirr for War ❖ 61
13. The 2020 US Presidential Race So Far ❖ 70
14. A Year of Decision ❖ 76
15. Wignat Whexit ❖ 81
16. Trump: Without Illusions or Apologies ❖ 86
17. Is America a Banana Republic Now? ❖ 91
18. After the Election ❖ 95
19. Goodbye, Mr. Trump ❖ 100

Free Speech Under Siege
20. Anarcho-Tyranny in Oslo ❖ 110
21. The Oslo Incident ❖ 121
22. The Norwegian Secret Police Order to Detain Greg Johnson ❖ 141

White Nationalism
23. Against White Nationalist Terrorism ❖ 149
24. Against Accelerationism ❖ 161
25. Epstein's Death & the Conspiracy Canard ❖ 166
26. The Paranoid Style in White Nationalism ❖ 177
27. Principles Are More Important Than People ❖ 184
28. The UK Voted for National Populism ❖ 193
29. The Groupie Question in White Nationalism ❖ 198
30. Our Votes Don't Matter, but Our Ideas Do ❖ 203

Index ❖ 209

About the Author ❖ 218

The Year America Died

Will future historians look back at 2020 and proclaim it the year America died? Maybe. But that's for future historians to decide. My thesis is different. For me, and for many other patriotic white Americans, 2020 definitely *felt* like the year America died.

Yes, the corpse of America is still shambling around on the world stage. In this respect, the presidency of senile Joe Biden and the speakership of taxidermized ghoul Nancy Pelosi are perfect symbolism. But the spirit of America has fled. Something different, something *alien* is animating America's corpse.

White Nationalists, of course, have known this for a long time. But now millions of patriotic Americans know it too. They *see* it. They are also looking for explanations and alternatives. This is a wonderful opportunity for our movement.

This volume is offered as food for thought, but I also hope it stirs up some righteous indignation and cements your resolve to do something constructive. It consists primarily of short, polemical commentaries on recent events from a White Nationalist point of view.

The essays in this volume were mostly written in 2020, although some were written in 2019 and 2021. That's because 2020 was a *long* year, just as historians speak of the "long nineteenth century" that ended in August 1914. I have also included a piece on the 2018 US midterm elections, just for context.

At the beginning of 2020, America was a very sick society, rotted by globalization, multiculturalism, and cultural decadence, and riven by a deep cultural and political polarization between the historic American nation—i.e., white America—and the American cultural and political establishment, including the rising tide of non-whites the establishment is championing to demographically swamp and replace white Americans.

Then, in 2020, America was hit by three crises. First, the COVID-19 pandemic killed hundreds of thousands of Americans and inflicted untold billions in economic damage, both directly and through bad political decisions. Second, an explosion of black and far-Left political violence in hundreds of cities and towns across America killed dozens and inflicted billions of dollars in damage to public and private property alike. Finally, Donald Trump was ousted in a blatantly fraudulent presidential election that has deepened political division and encumbered the Biden administration—and the whole political establishment, which either promoted or acquiesced to the fraud—with the stench of illegitimacy.

None of these crises is unprecedented. America has survived similar and worse problems. But America was younger and stronger then, and three crises at once might be too much for even a strong society. Will these crises be the end of America as we know it? It is too early to say. But we do know two things with certainty: Nothing lasts forever, and systems built on false principles and unsustainable practices are far more vulnerable to crises than systems founded on truth and sustainable practices.

These crises are by no means over, either.

Even in the best-case scenario, the American economy may take a long time to recover from COVID, if ever, and there are bound to be consequences for the orgy of COVID relief spending. And if COVID-19 is followed by COVID-21, COVID-22, *ad infinitum,* all bets are off.

Black Lives Matter and Leftists will continue to riot, which means that people will continue to die, cities will continue to burn, and crime will continue to soar. As COVID declines and travel opens up, prepare for mass exoduses of productive, law-abiding citizens from crime-ridden cities. Such depopulation will have enormous economic and cultural impacts for many years to come.

The pretexts for the riots are black criminals having frustrating encounters with the police or armed victims who fight back. There will always be crime. Thus there will always be black crime. In fact, because of BLM, there's a lot more of it. More black crime will lead to more frustrating encounters with police or victims. These encounters will spark more black rioting. Black rioting will lead to further decreased policing, which inevitably produces more black crime. Fortunately, this process cannot go on forever. It will simply continue until civilization collapses and every major city looks like Detroit.

Semi-retarded black criminals understand these incentives, which is why black crime is soaring. So it is impossible to believe that the establishment that promotes or acquiesces to such policies "know not what they do." They want this. They feel immune to any of the negative consequences that the rest of us suffer.

None of these crises will solve themselves. We need government action, specifically intelligent government action. But even if our government were predisposed to intelligent action, a divided and illegitimate government will not make the necessary course corrections to solve these problems, so they will only get worse.

I can't escape the conclusion that there is a great deal of suffering in store for America. It could have been avoided if people had listened to reason. But now the reckoning is upon us, and all we can do is make it count for something. These crises are an opportunity to loosen our enemies' grip on power, awaken white people to the depth of our plight, and offer them a workable alternative: populism not elitism, nationalism not globalism, truth and justice rather than political correctness, and homelands for all peoples rather than rootlessness, alienation, and "diversity." For a deeper understanding of what is wrong and what must be done, I recommend my earlier books *The White Nationalist Manifesto* and *White Identity Politics*.[1]

Acknowledgements

I want to thank the readers and supporters of *Counter-Currents* for making this book possible. I also want to thank Alex Graham, James O'Meara, Hyacinth Bouquet, Buttercup Dew, and Kevin Slaughter for their help in publishing this book.

The striking cover photo was taken on January 6, 2021, in Washington, D.C. It went viral on social media, but the original account that published it was deleted, so there was no way to determine the identity of the photographer. If you have any information, please write to me at editor@counter-currents.com.

This book is dedicated to Derek Chauvin, Ashli Babbitt, and Kyle Rittenhouse. They deserve justice. When white people have a country of our own, they'll get it.

August 4, 2021

---

[1] Greg Johnson, *The White Nationalist Manifesto* (San Francisco: Counter-Currents, 2018) and *White Identity Politics* (San Francisco: Counter-Currents, 2020)

How Covid-19 Will Change the World

I should have called this article, "How COVID-19 Could Change the World, If the Right Uses it Intelligently," but that isn't exactly elegant, and I had severely overestimated the Right.

Sadly, the Right-wing response to COVID was pretty much an intellectual and political disaster. In the United States, the Right is deeply infected by classical liberalism, which denies that there is a common good of society that trumps individual interests. Or, if classical liberals admit that a common good exists, they deny that that state power is the way to attain it. American classical liberals generally believe that the greatest threat to society is the state.

By contrast, for all its faults, the Left is willing to use state power to pursue the common good. This is one reason that the Left moves from triumph to triumph: the Left prizes state power while the Right prizes state impotence; the Left wants to gain power while the Right wants to get rid of it.

Thus the Right's response to mask mandates, social distancing, lockdowns, and travel restrictions was twofold: a lot of whining about "freedom," "burgers," and "pints" plus simple denial: denial that COVID exists, denial that it is a threat, denial of basic epidemiology and common sense, for instance, that increasing distance and reducing contact between people reduces the spread of viruses.

The Left denies biological race differences because they contradict egalitarianism. The classical liberal Right denies the existence of public goods and public crises—pandemics, pollution, overpopulation, man-made extinction of species—because they contradict individualism.

White advocates should be better than that. If you are concerned about the survival of the white race, then you are not a liberal individualist. You recognize that there are higher goods that should trump individual choices, for instance when it comes to sex and economics. If you see the folly of ignoring inconvenient truths about race, then you can't seriously believe we can do the same thing with epidemiology.

COVID-19 is going to change the world. I just hope that I live to see it, along with the people I care about. I call the COVID-19 the "globalvirus," because globalism is the underlying condition that made it all possible. Let's hope that the globalvirus stops in its tracks today. Nobody else gets sick. Every sick person recovers. What are the political lessons?

1. GLOBALISM IS BAD.

By globalism, I mean erasing national borders to ease the global movement of people and goods. It is possible to have national borders and international trade and travel, but nations need to regulate them for the common good of their peoples.

Globalists have not abolished all borders yet. But within the Schengen Zone, they have removed passport controls. Within the European Union, millions of people have moved to other countries for better wages and benefits. The US southern border has been porous for decades, allowing in tens of millions of illegal immigrants. Immigration fraud, visa overstays, and other forms of bureaucratic incompetence or sabotage effectively abolish borders as well throughout most of the West.

Beyond mass migration, cheap plane tickets encourage enormous amounts of short-term travel for business and pleasure. But easy global freedom of movement is not good once a pandemic starts. By seeking to abolish borders and nations, globalist ideologies are the equivalent of constructing a ship without different compartments in the hull. It makes it easier to move around when everything is going well. But when the ship hits an iceberg, there is nothing to impede catastrophic failure.

Borders still exist. What matters is the will to use them. To the extent that societies embrace globalist values, they will be slow to close their borders. Thus more of their people will sicken and die. The root of this hesitation is the conviction that closing borders is *wrong*.

Once these countries decide that border controls are prudent, they discover that they no longer have the personnel and procedures in place to effectively screen travelers, leading to long lines and crowding, which are ideal for spreading the virus, ensuring that more people sicken and die.

2. DEMOCRACY IS BAD.

Democracy encourages politicians to think only as far ahead as the next election. Since disasters happen only occasionally, every politician knows that they are unlikely to happen on his watch. Since politicians—especially national leaders—have short terms of office, it makes no sense for them to use their political capital planning for events far into the future, especially events that may never happen—especially when they are constantly distracted by current crises, which often result from the failure of their own predecessors to plan ahead.

It is fashionable now to deride the "deep state" for being democratically unaccountable bureaucrats. But in a democracy, only a democratically unaccountable permanent bureaucracy can engage in long-range planning to secure the future against preventable evils. I see no evidence that such a deep state even exists in America today. What we call the deep state are just short-sighted, ultra-partisan hysterics: liberal bureaucrats suffering from Trump Derangement Syndrome.

3. GLOBAL "FREE TRADE" IS BAD.

Life expectancies for white Americans are now declining, but not for the upper classes. America's wealth and power are increasingly concentrated in the hands of old people, who are taking more drugs than ever to extend their lives still further. Because businessmen care only about profit, not about the common good of society, and because the American political class no longer puts America First, the vast majority of pharmaceuticals that keep America's leaders alive are manufactured in China, a hostile global rival. *China is capable of blackmailing the United States by threatening to cut off pharmaceuticals.* The COVID-19 pandemic has finally made clear the utter stupidity of offshoring the manufacture of strategically necessary goods.

4. LIBERALISM IS BAD.

Classical political philosophy and untutored common sense recognize that a legitimate government looks out for the common good of a society. A government that serves the factional interests of the ruling class at the expense of the rest of society is morally no different than a foreign invader.

Liberalism, however, unhooks politics from the idea of the common good. Liberalism is the politics of individualism. Individualism declares that only the individual and his interests matter. The idea of the common good is denounced as "collectivism." Some liberals deny that the common good exists. Others deny that it can be known. Still others claim that the state cannot secure it, so we need to hope that it is secured as an unintended consequence of individual selfishness.

No society was founded on liberalism, not even the United States. No society can function based on liberalism. Liberalism depends on the social cohesion, public-spiritedness, and self-sacrifice of pre-liberal societies while it slowly dissolves them in the acid of individualism. Like a spendthrift squandering his inheritance, liberalism lives on the social capital built up by non-liberal societies.

It takes a long time to ruin a society, so in normal circumstances, liberals can get away with their self-indulgence and folly. Just as spending one's inheritance makes one feel prosperous in the short run, liberalism unleashes economic creativity which fools people into thinking that life is getting better as society decays around them.

But in a crisis like a pandemic, when people need to pull together and sacrifice for the common good, the more liberal a society is, the slower and more grudging the response. In normal times, liberalism encourages "Every man for himself." And in emergencies, liberalism encourages "Every man for himself." The more liberal a society, the more vulnerable it is to mass death in times of plague.

5. Diversity, Multiculturalism, Open Borders, & Anti-Racism Are Bad.

Today's Left promotes the fake moral absolute of "openness" to "otherness," from which they deduce such imperatives as diversity, multiculturalism, open borders, and anti-racism. Racism and xenophobia are thus absolute evils.

Thus as soon as the globalvirus cropped up, the Left created a moral panic about the dangers of "racism" and "xenophobia." Leftists are more concerned with protecting the Chinese from racism than with protecting their own neighbors from a deadly plague. Societies in which the Left is powerful will thus be more vulnerable to mass death in times of plague. But people in the grip of moral fanaticism can't see that.

Obviously, openness is not an absolute good if it allows in a plague. Which means there is *a good kind of xenophobia*, namely the xenophobia that protects us against the plague. There's *a good kind of racism*, namely the racism that protects us against the plague. After the globalvirus, charges of racism will no longer be moral kill shots. The proper response will be, "Yeah, but it is *the good kind* of racism—*the good kind* of xenophobia."

In times of plague, diversity and multiculturalism are dangerous burdens, for they decrease social trust and solidarity, which are necessary for disciplined and effective public health measures like quarantines, curfews, and testing.

6. Conservatism Is Bad.

Conservatism in America is just classical liberalism. In terms of their core convictions, significant numbers of American conservatives are simply libertarians who are morally opposed to any form of government intervention in the "free market." Even non-libertarian conservatives think primarily in terms of the economy. Furthermore, Donald Trump bet his reelection on a good economy, which means that his more cultish followers were highly invested in good economic news.

Thus American conservatives are more concerned with protecting the economy from "panic" over the globalvirus than protecting the American people from the virus itself.

The most astonishing thing about the globalvirus crisis is seeing how deep the free-market programming runs. Even putative nationalists have been running what

I call the "Republican dad script," minimizing the danger of the virus and worrying instead about protecting the economy from people who wish to protect their lives, and the lives of their loved ones. This "dad script" strikes me as equal parts alpha signaling and paternal concern for their stock portfolios.

Republicans are not unreasonable in their suspicion that the Left—including the mainstream media—are using the globalvirus against Trump. But that still doesn't mean it is not a serious health problem.

This kind of thinking has consequences. Polling data indicates that Republicans are significantly more likely to minimize the dangers of the globalvirus than Democrats, which means that Republicans, as well as their friends and families, are more likely to get sick and die. It also means that Republicans are more likely to support ineffectual or tardy responses to the crisis, which will ensure that more people die.

The market will come back. The people who will die because of Republican greed and complacency will be gone forever.

President Trump's initial response to the globalvirus was weak, probably for two reasons.

First, the Left was quick to stigmatize basic, commonsense preventative measures as "racism." Unfortunately, Trump and the Republican Party are unwilling to challenge the fake moral absolutes of the Left. Instead, they think it is clever to argue that the Democrats are the real racists.

Second, in order to work with Republicans, Trump has increasingly adopted their agenda, betting his reelection almost entirely on a strong economy. Thus when the globalvirus first hit, he was less concerned with protecting the American people from the virus than the economy. Fortunately, it looks like more sensible voices have prevailed.

Even if the globalvirus stops today, we are looking at a world in which nationalism is stronger and the anti-nationalist forces of globalism, democracy, liberalism, conservatism, and the diversity cult are weaker. So stay safe, stay sane, and let's hope we are all around to enjoy it.

Counter-Currents, March 18, 2020

I'm Changing My Tune About COVID-19

The COVID-19 pandemic is a complex and changing phenomenon, and so are my thoughts about it.

I can sympathize with the ecologists who think that the Earth has far too many humans and would welcome a pandemic to dramatically reduce our numbers. But not yet. This is not the time, because COVID-19 isn't the killer they've been hoping for, and as a member of a race that is already on the path to extinction—extinction as the predictable consequence of political policies and thus genocide—I am fighting for my race against its enemies, not for the planet against humanity.

COVID-19 presents national populists with remarkable metapolitical and political opportunities. So much so, that I have taken to calling it the "globalvirus." The globalvirus demonstrates that global capitalism, open borders, liberal individualism, multiculturalism, xenophilia, and democracy make nations more vulnerable to deadly pandemics. The countries with protectionist economies, real borders, a commitment to the common good, ethnic homogeneity, healthy xenophobia, and more "authoritarian" regimes are less vulnerable.

COVID-19 has also discredited most of what passes for the Right today in Western societies: namely, various forms of classical liberalism. Classical liberalism comes in two varieties: the moderate and extreme.

The moderate classical liberals are your mainstream Republicans who identify not with America but with capitalism. Their first reaction to the globalvirus was to deny it, because they did not want to interrupt the economy. I'm sure it occurred to them that the globalvirus might well kill a lot of people in America, as it did in China and

Italy and Spain. But, in their heart of hearts, these people were gambling that *other* people would die—old people, poor people, etc.—and they deemed this a small price (for others) to pay to preserve the value of their stock portfolios.

But at least moderate classical liberals believe that there are some circumstances in which government action is legitimate, for instance to bail out big business or to defend the borders of Israel. Thus, reluctantly, some of these people might actually be wrangled into doing something for the American people.

Extreme classical liberals don't believe it is legitimate for the government to do anything for the common good, because they don't believe that collectives exist or have interests that are legitimately pursued by the state. Thus their reaction to the globalvirus is the same as their reaction to any other collective problem: simple denial. Denialism comes in two flavors: vanilla economism and tutti frutti conspiracy theories.

Since we have a Republican administration, when intelligence reports about the globalvirus outbreak in China started coming in as early as November, they fell on deaf ears. Apparently there was not a single populist who cared about the American people anywhere to be found in the Trump administration, just business boosters who wanted to protect the economy from people who feared drowning in their own bodily fluids. And, because Republicans are not just greedy and stupid but also cowardly, they were well aware that any attempt to restrict travel from China would be decried as "racism" by the Left. Hence they decided to go with the "It's just the flu, bro" narrative.

If Hillary Clinton were in office, the result would have been exactly the same, because she is 100% owned by the oligarchy. Her rationalizations would simply have put greater emphasis on anti-racism.

If the United States had a national populist government that put America first, we might have been spared the human and economic costs of the pandemic by simply locking down travel and screening all people coming from outside the country. But the travel restrictions adopted were too little, too late, and once a certain number of carriers had entered the United States, we only had two choices.

Plan A is to do nothing, in which case millions might get sick, hundreds of thousands might die, and national life, including the economy, would be devastated. Plan B is to shut down the spread of the virus, in which case far fewer people would sicken and die and the nation, including economic life, would bounce back more quickly. The Trump administration adopted Plan B, but an astonishing number of Republicans would have given us Plan A. That is something we national populists should never forget and never forgive.

Once Plan B was rolled out, the US government needed to mitigate the economic and social costs. I grade their performance D-minus. The establishment that created the crisis by dragging its feet—out of Republican Mammonism and Democratic xenophilia—delivered exactly the relief package you would expect: massive bailouts to big business, massive giveaways to non-whites, and $1,200 and some trickle-down for average white Americans, millions of whom lost their jobs.

But the mere fact that millions of Americans had been thrown out of work was not enough to stop the Right from importing more cheap labor or the Left from importing more refugees. Nor was the shortage of protective face masks enough to stop the US from allowing millions to be bought up and exported by foreigners or simply *given* to Israel. Our rulers are so committed to replacing Americans with foreigners that *they won't even pretend to put Americans first in a national crisis,* and not just any national crisis, one that falls *in an election year*. They can't help it. It's just their nature.

I have no idea how long this pandemic will last and what it will cost in human lives and social, political, and economic chaos. Neither do any of the experts.

But I am certain of one thing. The pandemic will end. Which means that there will be a time when it is right to say "It's over. Let's start living again." When that happens, the accusation that "Republicans are just putting profits over people" will no longer be true. It will be just cheap demagoguery.

Human knowledge is finite. Even the most objective analysts can never reliably call the top or the bottom of curves. And all people have biases. Republicans—whose bias is toward normalcy, complacency, and GDP—will always jump the gun on the back to work date. Democrats—who are addicted to moral indignation and desperate to attack Republicans from every angle—will be ranting about "profits over people" long after the discard date.

National populists shouldn't follow them. That's why I am planning to change my tune.

Of course, things will never really go back to normal. We national populists can't allow that. It is up to national populists to make sure that *the new normal* incorporates the lessons of the pandemic. We need to manufacture strategic products in our own countries, including drugs and medical equipment. We need paid sick leave for all employees. We need real borders. We need travel bans from plague zones and medical screenings and quarantines for nationals returning home. We need more expensive and less frequent air travel, but we can cushion the impact on the airlines with tens of millions of deportation flights. We need to rebuild social trust and solidarity, so people are willing to sacrifice for the common good. We need a leadership caste that puts our people first and lays plans to do so far into the future.

Unless COVID-19 becomes extinct like smallpox, it will

also be part of the new normal. Every year, tens of thousands of Americans die in car accidents. But we don't stop driving, because these deaths are "normal." Every year, tens of thousands of Americans die of the flu and pneumonia. But we don't shut down society, because these deaths are "normal." We factor them in. They are "part of the plan." I'd like to reduce all these numbers. But none of them will fall to zero. You see, *death* is normal. There will never be a day when we run out of things to die from.

Once we get used to the globalvirus, it will be "part of the plan" as well. But that is not an argument to be complacent about the globalvirus today. We need to do our best to destroy this virus before there is any talk of living with it. Nor is it an argument for complacency in the future, because anticipating and mitigating new pandemics should be "part of the plan" as well.

Since the globalvirus pandemic is complex and constantly changing, practically everyone will be right about it at one time or another. But at present practically everyone is wrong because their timing is off. "Interesting times," indeed.

Counter-Currents, April 9, 2020

BLACK LIES MATTER

The most depressing thing about Black Lives Matter is that the entire movement is based upon blatant and easily exposed lies—yet none of that seems to matter to our leaders. BLM flourishes—and American cities burn—because the press, politicians, and corporate elites either actively promote black lies—or they are just too weak and cowardly to resist them. America is falling apart because among its leaders, the best lack all conviction while the worst are full of passionate intensity.

Thus America desperately needs new leadership. The number one criterion for the job is to speak the truth about the people who are destroying the country. As Jef Costello put it, we've got to "Speak the Truth or Kiss It All Goodbye."[1]

Black Lie #1: BLM martyrs Trayvon Martin, Michael Brown, George Floyd, etc. were innocent victims of "white racism."

This is a double lie.

First, there is no evidence that "white racism" played any role in any of these incidents. What would such a racist incident even look like? Do people seriously believe that all of these men were singled out and killed "just because they were black"? That's simply not true. A black man can be arrested with a bloody machete in his hand, and his first reaction will be to accuse the police of singling him out "just because he's black."

Yes, it really is that childish. Such accusations should be greeted with laughter and derision, not piously echoed by the press and social media platforms. That goes double

---

[1] Jef Costello, "Speak the Truth or Kiss It All Goodbye," *Counter-Currents*, June 8, 2020.

for people who think racism is a serious problem, since false and silly charges of racism make people less receptive to real cases.

Furthermore, Martin, Brown, Floyd etc. all ended up dead because they were far from "innocent." They were up to no good. Trayvon Martin assaulted George Zimmerman, putting him in fear for his life, which entitled Zimmerman to use lethal force in self-defense. Michael Brown tried to grab a police officer's gun, which entitled the officer to use lethal force in self-defense. George Floyd was high as a kite, sitting in the driver's seat of a car, when he was approached by the police for passing a counterfeit bill. Floyd then died of a drug overdose while resisting arrest. Dying is a likely consequence when one assaults men with guns or takes lethal doses of drugs. These men were not victims of white racism. They were victims of their own bad decisions.

The reason why any number of other black men in the vicinity didn't end up dead like Martin, Brown, and Floyd is that most of these men *actually were innocent of wrongdoing*. Unlike Martin, Brown, and Floyd, they really dindu nuffin. Yet the message of BLM is that any black man, guilty or innocent, is always moments away from being murdered by white police. They tell that lie to create permanent, festering racial resentment. It is also an inversion of the truth, since the vast majority of black murder victims are killed by other blacks. Blacks are safer around whites than around other blacks.

In the cases of Trayvon Martin and George Floyd, attributing their deaths to "white racism" is a triple lie, because George Zimmerman and half of the officers who tried to arrest Floyd were not even white. Those are pretty big facts to overlook. How did they slip by legions of "investigative journalists," "fact-checkers," and social media censorship algorithms? Because such facts don't matter if one's overriding goal is not to report the truth but to inflame anti-white hatred.

Black Lie #2: American police are particularly dangerous to blacks.

Americans who listen to the mass media are convinced that hundreds, if not thousands, of blacks are killed every year by police. We are breathlessly told that, despite being only 13% percent of the population, blacks were 23.4% of the people shot to death by police in 2019, 23.6% of those killed in 2020—and the number could be higher, because the race of more than 10% of the victims is unknown.[2] It sounds damning, but the claim that American police are particularly dangerous to blacks is a double lie.

First, I have a "despite being 13% of the population" statistic of my own: despite being 13% of the population, blacks are responsible for around 50% of violent crime.[3] If police are doing their jobs, that means that blacks are likely to come into contact with police investigating half of all violent crimes. When violent criminals encounter the police, they are far more likely to violently resist arrest, for two main reasons: violence comes easy to them and the consequences of being arrested are more severe. Given that, the fact that blacks are less than a quarter of the people shot to death by police seems shockingly *low*. It certainly does not prove that police are overzealous in policing blacks. If anything, it indicates that they are shockingly lax and diffident.

There are figures about how many unarmed blacks are killed by police every year. For instance, in 2019, the number was not 1,000 or 100. It was ten, and as Tucker Carlson reported, in virtually every case, the blacks were assaulting

---

[2] Number of people shot to death by the police in the United States from 2017 to 2021, by race, Statista.com.

[3] Steve Sailer, "FBI: Blacks Made Up 55.9% of Known Murder Offenders in 2019," *The Unz Review*, September 29, 2020.

police.⁴ The FBI reports that in 2019, 48 police officers died as a result of felonious acts while doing their duties.⁵ The FBI offers the racial breakdown of the dead officers (40 were white), but they don't inform us of the races of the killers. However, the FBI reports that in the cases of 511 police officers killed between 2004 and 2013, 43% of the killers were black—despite being merely 13% of the overall population.⁶ So if blacks are less than a quarter of the people killed by cops, and more than 40% of cop killers, the truth is exactly the reverse of BLM's message. *Blacks are far more dangerous to police than police are to blacks.*

Second, if blacks are killed by the police at about half the rate they commit violent crimes, one has to ask: What racial groups are *overrepresented* among police killings? It turns out that whites are. As Richard Houck ably documents, whites are stopped, ticketed, arrested, and killed by police at a higher rate than they actually commit crimes, while blacks are *under*-policed in all these categories.⁷ *Police are significantly more dangerous to whites than to blacks.* This is in spite of the fact that the vast majority of police in America are white.

Why? Because the police are government employees, thus it makes sense that their work reflects the pervasive anti-white biases of our hostile elite. Beyond that, black grievance politics—including Black Lives Matter—surely plays a huge role in this.

Why do black agitators champion the causes of flagrant black criminals? Because they want to make it easier

---

⁴ Tucker Carlson, "Is America being torn apart by a total, complete–but provable–lie?," Foxnews.com, June 4, 2020.

⁵ FBI Releases 2019 Statistics on Law Enforcement Officers Killed in the Line of Duty, FBI.gov, May 4, 2020.

⁶ Michelle Ye Hee Lee, "Are black or white offenders more likely to kill police?," *Washington Post*, January 8, 2015.

⁷ Richard Houck, "Law Enforcement and the Hostile Elite," *Counter-Currents*, June 20, 2018.

for blacks to commit crimes and more dangerous for police to stop them. Once those incentives are in place, it doesn't take a genius to predict the consequences. If you make it safer for blacks to commit crime, you'll get more black crime.

But if police are turning a blind eye to black criminals, they are turning a jaundiced eye on whites. They've got to arrest someone, and what better way to prove that they are good anti-racists than to over-zealously police white people?

We really do need a national conversation about systemic racism in American law enforcement. But contrary to BLM, *American law enforcement is systemically racist against whites and for blacks.*

Counter-Currents, May 17, 2021

Do Black Lives Matter?

When protesters began chanting "Black Lives Matter," my first reaction was disgust at the brazen effrontery of that slogan. Imagine a movement to legalize pedophilia calling itself "We Love Kids." Nobody disagrees with loving kids in the abstract, but most people oppose letting perverts get away with raping them. Calling such a movement "We Love Kids" puts critics at a disadvantage when they have to begin, "Yes, we love kids too, but . . ."

The same is true of Black Lives Matter. Black Lives Matter should be called Black Thugs Matter. BLM does not champion black victims of black crime. It does not rally to stop blacks from killing themselves with drugs, alcohol, and menthols. It does not try to protect blacks from vicious dogs, abortionists, incompetent doctors, or abusive nursing home staffers. BLM's principal activity is rioting when black criminals die in encounters with the police or victims who fight back.

BLM's goal is to make it safer for blacks to commit crimes and more dangerous for cops to arrest them. The entirely predictable and obvious outcome of BLM's efforts is more black crime. Politicians and reporters with above-average IQs pretend not to understand this. But black thugs with IQs of 85 understand incentives. So do policemen. The result has been an explosion of violence that Heather MacDonald has labeled "the Ferguson effect."[1] It should simply be called the Black Lives Matter effect.

"Black Lives Matter" has turned out to be a very expensive, destructive, and deadly slogan. Thus we have to screw up our courage to question it. Yet not even the most cold-hearted racist would flatly deny that "black lives mat-

---

[1] Heather Mac Donald, "The Ferguson Effect," *Washington Post*, July 21, 2016.

ter." Even people who think blacks are a cancer on the planet still grant that their lives matter to *someone*. Even though I don't want to share a country with black people, I still think their lives matter enough to have basic human rights.

So how do you respond to the assertion that black lives matter?

If you take the "yes, but . . ." approach, you'd better make it count: "Yes, 'black lives matter,' but . . . some lives matter more than others. Trayvon Martin, Michael Brown, Ahmaud Arbery, George Floyd, and other BLM martyrs were criminal scum. Their lives matter less than the lives of the good people they victimized. If you champion such trash, you're either stupid, crazy, or evil." I'm betting BLM's leaders are evil. They are cynics trying to gaslight morons into acts of violence or guilt-trip them into giveaways.

A better approach is simply to challenge the assertion. Ask them "*Do* black lives really matter?" Ask them for evidence. Ask them for clarification. Don't let "Black Lives Matter" remain a simple categorical statement. It is formulated that way to make it difficult to reject. Ask "*How much* do black lives matter?" and "*To whom* do black lives matter?" "Do black lives matter *more* than other lives, such that blacks can victimize other groups with impunity?" "Do other things, like justice, matter more than black lives?"

BLM supporters will just start shrieking. All they have is shrieking. Since their entire movement is based on lies, heinous double standards, and the willingness of whites to patronize and tolerate their infantile babble, BLM can't afford to have a single civil and intelligent conversation, lest their entire movement collapse.

But it is worth triggering some shrieking. You won't find it edifying, but many in your audience will. Even if it be only silently, in the privacy of their own thoughts, many of them will draw the conclusion "They've got nothing" then quietly back away.

It doesn't make you a bad person to question the slogan "Black Lives Matter." After all, *black lives don't even seem to matter to the movement calling itself Black Lives Matter*. BLM's goal is to make it safer for blacks to commit crimes. The principal victims of black criminals are other blacks. Apparently these black lives don't matter. *Black lives only matter to BLM if they can be weaponized against whites*. In a sense, *only white lives matter to BLM*, because black lives matter to them merely as a way of getting whitey.

If the slogan "Black Lives Matter" means anything, it means "Black lives don't matter enough *to white people*." But that's a complete falsehood. In truth, black lives don't matter much to black people in general or to BLM in particular. In fact, *white people tend to value black lives more than black people do*.

What counts as evidence that black lives don't matter enough to white people? Pretty much any bad outcome for blacks is blamed on whites. If black people are overrepresented among criminals and underrepresented among inventors, that's the fault of white people. If blacks are overrepresented among the poor and underrepresented among the rich, that's white people's fault as well. If black children suffer more from illegitimacy, absent fathers, and child abuse than white children, white people are to blame for that too. If white people *cared more*—if black lives *mattered more* to them—these inequities would disappear, because racial inequalities are not based on nature. Nor are they based on the choices of blacks themselves. They are based simply on white social arrangements, at the bottom of which are white ill will and indifference toward blacks.

Note that BLM's accusation assumes that—like children and pets—blacks have no agency or responsibility when bad things happen to them. Why are children abused? Because adults don't value their lives enough. Why are pets abused? Because their owners don't value their lives enough. Why do black people suffer? Because white people don't think that black lives matter enough. Note also that white people—like parents or pet owners—are attributed complete agency and responsibility when it comes to the well-being of their wards.

But if white people are somehow collectively responsible for George Floyd's death, why are we not responsible for Oprah Winfrey's success? Of course, blacks do not wish to surrender *all* agency and responsibility to white people. They are happy to take credit for good things that happen to them. Indeed, they are happy to take credit for good things that other people do as well, such as building the pyramids. Whites are responsible only for black failings, not for black achievements. We deserve only blame, never thanks.

It is childish for blacks to take credit for the things that please them while blaming their suffering on whites. But denying all moral agency to blacks is not entirely absurd. First, the average black American has an IQ of 85. Very large numbers of black Americans have IQs of 70 or below, which for white people is the cut-off for mental retardation. They are adults with the minds of children and thus should not be held responsible under the law. Second, large numbers of blacks are incarcerated for crimes, during which time they are wards of the state. So is it really such a stretch for white people to take complete responsibility for blacks in America? Isn't this what BLM is basically demanding? And doesn't it cohere nicely with white liberal paternalism toward blacks? Aren't American policies toward blacks basically a glorified form of babysitting?

But I don't think BLM has really thought this through. As I already pointed out, blacks only want to be absolved of blame and punishments, not praise and rewards. Beyond that, if whites take full responsibility for blacks, we need to make their decisions for them, just as we do for children. But what if they complain? So what? They aren't legal adults, so as long as something is in their best interest, their consent is neither possible nor necessary.

Of course, on this scenario, black consent would also not be required if whites decided that racial separation is best for everyone and resolved to send black Americans to their own homeland. I personally prefer offering blacks incentives to voluntarily separate, but I admit that making them wards of the state would certainly expedite the process.

It is easy to establish that black people hold their lives rather cheap. Despite being 13% of the US population, blacks have long committed 50% or more of the murders. Based on the FBI's 2019 statistics, blacks committed 55.9% of murders.[2] As Barack Obama might say, they are sucker-punching above their weight. Because of the collapse of policing due to Black Lives Matter in 2020, murders have skyrocketed in black areas (gun murders up 34.4%), so the 2020 statistics will likely be much higher.[3]

The vast majority of black murderers pick black victims, even though blacks are also far more likely to murder whites than whites are to murder blacks: blacks were 54.7% of murder victims in 2019;[4] in 2018, 70.3% of black homicide victims were killed by other blacks, while only 10.6% were killed by whites;[5] in the same year, 15% of

---

[2] Expanded Homicide, 2019 Crime in the United States, FBI.gov.

[3] Steve Sailer, "The Future of Floydism," *Taki's Magazine*, May 25, 2021.

[4] Expanded Homicide, 2019 Crime in the United States, FBI.gov.

[5] Rachel E. Morgan, Ph.D., and Barbara A. Oudekerk, Criminal Victimization, 2018, U.S. Department of Justice, Office of Justice Programs, Bureau of Justice Statistics, September 2019.

white murder victims were killed by blacks;[6] this is despite the fact that the white population is more than five times the size of the black population. Obviously, black people hold other black lives very cheap.

But those are *other* black lives. Surely black people hold *their own* lives very dear.

No, not really. Blacks suffer from high rates of crime, poverty, drug- and alcohol-related problems, unplanned pregnancies, sexually transmitted diseases, and general proneness to accidents. All of these problems spring, in part, from a tendency to focus too much on the present and ignore the future. Economists and psychologists call discounting the future for present pleasures "high time preferences." Black high time preferences are well-documented across the board.[7] High time preferences amount to a form of heedlessness of the long-term consequences of present-day actions, which means that one's one future—one's own life outside the present—matters less than momentary pleasures in the now.

But there's no need to approach this in such abstract terms. Let's look at BLM's alleged martyrs. How much did Trayvon Martin's life matter *to him* when he assaulted a man with a gun? How much did Michael Brown's life matter *to him* when he tried to take a gun from the hands of a police officer? How much did Ahmaud Arbery's life matter *to him* when he tried to wrestle a shotgun out of another man's hands? What is it with blacks taking bare hands to a gunfight? Assaulting an armed man is a form of suicidal behavior. How much do the lives of suicidal people matter *to them*?

Isn't there something grotesque about the cult that has grown up around George Floyd? After all, Floyd was a ca-

---

[6] Ibid.

[7] See the appendix on "Time Preferences" in Michael Levin, *Why Race Matters* (Oakton, Virginia: New Century Books, 2016).

reer criminal and a drug abuser. He also fathered and abandoned at least five children with various women. At the time of his death, he was walking around with COVID-19. These behaviors reveal that Floyd rated present pleasures very highly while holding the lives of others, as well as his own long-term survival, very cheap. Floyd died because he was high on methamphetamine and fentanyl, capering around a store with a banana in his hand, trying to pass a counterfeit $20 bill. When police approached him as he sat behind the wheel of a car that he was too stoned to drive safely, he gobbled down even more drugs, dying of an overdose while being restrained for resisting arrest. Floyd was not murdered. He died of the predictable consequences of his own bad decisions. Taking a lethal dose of meth and fentanyl is suicidal behavior, as is resisting arrest. If George Floyd's life mattered more to him, he would be alive today.

You people treating George Floyd as a saint look like fools. At best, you are fools. At worst, you are cynics manipulating fools to benefit yourselves while harming society as a whole. You're probably too stupid, crazy, or evil to be trusted with any civic responsibilities. I'd take away your votes at the very least.

That's why I regard the slogan "Black Lives Matter" with such disgust. Why should any of these phony BLM martyrs' lives matter more to me than they mattered to themselves? *Why should black lives matter more to whites than they do to black people?*

When people engage in suicidal behavior, we assume that they are out of their minds and feel entitled to intervene. When that happens, we feel quite self-righteous about the fact that these people's lives matter more to us than to them. We are operating, however, on the assumption that we are dealing with a psychological emergency. When the emergency is over and the victim is back in his right mind, we can end our paternalistic intervention and go back to normal.

But what if it is *normal* for whites and blacks to value black lives differently? What if black lives will *always* matter more to us than to blacks themselves? Do we really want to commit ourselves to a *permanent* state of emergency, to *permanent* paternalism, to *permanent* babysitting? Isn't there something presumptuous and ethnocentric for whites to declare that we, not blacks, are the arbiters of how much black lives matter? Isn't this just another version of benevolent colonialism, what Kipling called "the white man's burden"? Don't you think that blacks would eventually find such a situation oppressive? In fact, they already do.

But the only way to stop "oppressing" blacks is to abandon civilized—i.e., white—standards of behavior. That is, in effect, what BLM has already accomplished. The results are clear: a crime wave in black neighborhoods, increasingly numerous and savage black attacks on whites, and the abandonment of fair trials, e.g., the open intimidation of a jury into convicting Derek Chauvin. Eventually, it will dawn on even liberal whites that blacks are a retarding force in civilization. White Nationalists reached that conclusion a long time ago.

Fortunately, there is a solution. Whites and blacks in America have irreconcilable differences. When a married couple has such differences, the solution is divorce. After four centuries of racial conflict and resentment in America, we need to start listening to reason rather than hope. It is time for blacks and whites to seek a racial divorce.[8] We need separate, independent nations for blacks and whites in North America.

Counter-Currents, June 11, 2021

---

[8] Greg Johnson, "Irreconcilable Differences: The Case for Racial Divorce," *Truth, Justice, & a Nice White Country* (San Francisco: Counter-Currents, 2015).

George Floyd Got Justice

The cries for justice over the deaths of Trayvon Martin and Michael Brown were hoaxes. Both men were criminals who died because they were dumb enough to assault men with guns. The same is true of Ahmaud Arbery.

They got justice.

Jussie Smollet and Bubba Wallace were hoaxers painting themselves as victims of hate crimes. But fake hate crimes against non-whites are real hate crimes against whites. Both men's careers should be canceled, and they should end up in jail for their crimes.

There are more than forty million black people in America. Can't Black Lives Matter find at least *one* actual victim of racism?

Now, with the leak of the police body-camera footage of the arrest of George Floyd, we have confirmation of what sensible people suspected all along: George Floyd was not a victim of police brutality or injustice.

We were sold the story that, for no good reason, Floyd was thrown to the ground by a brutal cop, Derek Chauvin, who then put his knee on Floyd's neck for nearly nine minutes while Floyd pleaded that he could not breathe, choking him to death.

Based on this story, Derek Chauvin was fired and indicted for murder, and the three other cops who assisted him were fired and indicted for aiding and abetting murder.

Also based on this story, America has been convulsed by more than two months of race riots, which have killed dozens, injured countless others, and destroyed billions of dollars in property and countless livelihoods.

There were many facts that did not fit this story, however.

George Floyd's autopsy revealed that he wasn't suffocated. Instead, he died of heart failure. He was suffering from heart disease and COVID-19. He also had the opioid fentanyl in his system as well as methamphetamine. The medical examiner said these drugs contributed to this death. (He also had traces of cannabis.)

Beyond that, Floyd was apprehended before he could drive off, clearly intoxicated, after trying to pass a counterfeit $20 bill. Should the police have allowed him to just drive away? Obviously not. They had to do something to get Floyd out of his car and away from the public so he could not endanger himself or others.

The person who called the police reported that Floyd was acting strangely, which in all likelihood meant that he was intoxicated or mentally ill, thus not to be trifled with.

It turns out that Floyd had a long criminal record, including an armed robbery in which held a gun to the stomach of a pregnant woman. In short, George Floyd was a real piece of shit.

Moreover, putting a knee on an uncooperative suspect's neck is an approved police control technique, so how could Chauvin be indicted for murder?

Finally, there was never any evidence that *race* played any role in Floyd's death. He was not arrested because he was black, but because he committed a crime. He was not forcibly restrained because he was black, but because he was uncooperative. Two of the four officers were non-white. The claim that race had anything to do with Floyd's death at all was simply *a baseless assertion* amplified and endlessly repeated by the media and BLM agitators.

But now we *know* that it was all a fraud. What does the police body camera footage reveal?

First of all, it reveals that George Floyd was dishonest, uncooperative, and acted deranged and scary.

- ❖ Floyd claimed that he had just lost his mother (he hadn't).

- He claimed to be too claustrophobic to get in the police car, which was a lie because he was not too claustrophobic to sit in his own car.
- He claimed twice that he was not on drugs, falsely.
- He refused repeatedly to allow the police to cuff him.
- He refused repeatedly to get in the police car.
- He claimed multiple times that he could not breathe *before* he ended up on the ground with Chauvin's knee on his neck. Obviously he was lying before that, so it made sense for Chauvin to disbelieve him when Floyd was on the ground. And, in any case, remember that the medical examiner said Floyd did not die of asphyxiation.

Second, the video reveals that the police dealt with Floyd with a level of patience and professionalism that I certainly could not have mustered. One cannot say that Chauvin lost his patience or lashed out at Floyd.

Ask yourself, dear reader, would you have been able to maintain *your* cool in the same situation? I know I would have snapped. I was thinking "Can't we just arm police with tranquilizer darts to bring these beasts down?" This video gives me nothing but respect for the police who have to deal day in and day out with deranged criminals like George Floyd.

Was George Floyd a victim of injustice? No, he died because (1) he committed a crime, (2) refused to comply with the police, and (3) was so high on drugs that he was not up to the rigors of being forcibly arrested. If he hadn't done any of those things, he—and a lot of other people—would still be alive today.

George Floyd's death was *entirely* his fault. It wasn't murder. It was the predictable result of Floyd's own bad character and bad choices. It was his just deserts.

George Floyd got justice.

Now we have to secure justice for Derek Chauvin and his fellow officers, as well as for the millions of Americans whose lives have been turned upside down by this massive hoax perpetrated by the government of Minneapolis, the State of Minnesota, Black Lives Matter, the mainstream media, and the far Left—aided and abetted by the craven eunuchs of the mainstream Right.

If I were Donald Trump, I would invoke the Insurrection Act, then spend the next few weeks arresting the leaders of BLM and antifa, as well as their collaborators in state and municipal governments, for the crimes they have already committed. Once the Leftist beast is decapitated, I would pardon Derek Chauvin and his fellow officers. Then I'd grab some popcorn.

"But we could never do that! Blacks would burn the country down!"

If that is your initial reaction, I want you to reflect on it. Derek Chauvin, his fellow officers, and the whole planet have been victimized by a blatant hoax. If we can't do the right thing and call a stop to it, then aren't we admitting that *we have to choose between having justice and having black people in America*? Well I choose justice. Which is reason number one-hundred-million-and-one why I believe that blacks and whites in America need to go our separate ways. We need a racial divorce.

Counter-Currents, August 6, 2020

Verdict on America

Officer Derek Chauvin should not have been convicted for murder in the death of George Floyd. But the conviction comes as no surprise, because it comes at the end of a long list of things that shouldn't have happened.

Chauvin never should have been tried in the first place. No crime was committed. Chauvin was merely in the wrong place at the wrong time when a habitual criminal and druggie finally overdosed. If Chauvin had done nothing, Floyd may have lost consciousness while driving his car, possibly taking his passengers and random innocents with him. Chauvin did his job, which was to protect the public. His life was ruined for it, with little thought for the message that this sends to other cops and other criminals.

Floyd's death should never have been turned into a racial incident in the first place. There was no evidence that racial hatred or prejudice played any role in Chauvin's actions. He didn't decide to kill a random black man. He responded to a crime committed by a black man. Black men come to the attention of the police so often because they commit crimes far in excess of their percentage of the overall American population. Furthermore, whites are more likely to suffer from police brutality than blacks.

Derek Chauvin was not a racist cop. Nor did he act like one. We must note, however, that George Floyd did act like a walking stereotype: overdosing on multiple drugs, passing counterfeit currency, and prancing about with a banana in his hand. When he was confronted by the police, he lied, whined, and generally refused to take responsibility for his actions. George Floyd's life obviously didn't matter that much to him. So why should it matter to the rest of us?

Derek Chauvin was tried to appease a mob of violent morons foaming at the mouth from an overdose of media lies and anti-white hate. He was lynched in the court of public opinion, long before he had his day in court. There was probably not a place in America where Chauvin could have gotten a fair trial, but he certainly should not have been tried in Minneapolis. The jurors certainly should have been sequestered. Countless public officials—including such walking stereotypes as Minneapolis Mayor Jacob Frey and Representative Maxine Waters—should not have abandoned the presumption of innocence and declared Chauvin guilty of murder. And, of course, the domestic terrorist groups BLM and antifa should have been mercilessly crushed by the police long before they could threaten violence if Chauvin were acquitted.

Why do we have government in the first place? To secure justice. Why do we give public officials power and prestige? So they secure justice not just when it is easy but especially when it is *hard*, even when it requires saying "no" to angry lynch mobs.

But given that the entire political establishment defaulted on its duty to say "no" to the mob—when they weren't actively encouraging or even joining them—it was too much to expect twelve jurors in Minneapolis to finally stand up for truth and justice.

Given that the entire political system made a farce of the trial before it even convened, why would we expect twelve ordinary people to do the right thing? After all, the whole purpose of having a justice system is so that ordinary people don't have to take justice into their own hands.

One could argue, of course, that the jurors are *part* of the justice system. They had oaths to uphold. But as the trial progressed, it quickly became clear to even the dimmest juror that Derek Chauvin was on trial merely for doing his sworn duty as part of the justice system. And if the system would throw a police officer to the mob to appease them, what chance would the jury have?

The Chauvin verdict is a verdict on the American justice system. From top to bottom, it has failed. You can pursue justice or pander to morons, but you can't do both.

Of course Chauvin has the right to appeal. But that does not change the fact that he should never have been tried in the first place. Even if Chauvin had been acquitted, his life has been turned upside down. Even if Chauvin's conviction is overturned on appeal, he will never get justice at this point. One would have to sack and prosecute countless public officials and members of the press to make even a dent in the massive hoax crime that has been committed against Derek Chauvin and the American people at large.

Derek Chauvin was convicted because of the threat of massive BLM and antifa violence if he were acquitted. A serious country would never have allowed this, since convicting Chauvin will produce more violence than acquitting him.

Even dumb animals respond to incentives. So do terrorists, criminals, and cops. Convicting Chauvin rewards political violence. Rewarding violence produces more of it. A serious country would have dismantled BLM and antifa for being domestic terrorist organizations long ago. Furthermore, BLM's basic demand is to make it safer for blacks to commit crimes and more dangerous for police to arrest them. The result is predictable: soaring black crime.

Civilization is a fragile thing. It depends on the forces of order constantly repressing the forces of chaos. Civilized people are soft-hearted. They don't like seeing the knee of order on the neck of chaos. They'll like it even less when the knee is removed.

Want to destroy civilization? Just make crime legal. The criminals will do the rest.

What should white normies do?

Batten down, because a great wave of chaos is coming, and your skin will be your uniform. You may not want colored people as your enemies, but sometimes your enemies choose you. Your head may be overflowing with white guilt and good intentions, but the only thing the mob will see is the color of your skin. Your fake woke virtues will not save you.

What should white advocates do?

First, take sensible precautions to secure your personal safety and the safety of your loved ones, but be warned that even violence in self-defense will be prosecuted.

Second, don't call for violence or engage in it. Even as blacks and communists are trashing America, the establishment is looking for white racists to blame. Don't play along with them.

Third, use this as an opportunity to educate. I didn't know whether Chauvin would be convicted or acquitted, but I did know in advance that there would be violence either way. Furthermore, I knew it would demonstrate that America has to choose between justice and pandering to black people. This entire farce is built on lies and enabled by viciousness and cowardice. It is a crushing indictment of multiculturalism, the liberals who promote it, and the conservative cowards who enable them. If we can't use this to wake people up, we aren't worth our salt.

Take heart, though. Most whites already know this is a farce, but they aren't quite sure what to do about it. So just repeat the same basic mantras: We shouldn't have to live this way. If white people had a country of our own, this would not be happening. We can't live with these people, but we can live without them. We have irreconcilable differences. It is time for a racial divorce.

Counter-Currents, April 21, 2021

AMNESTY YOUR ANCESTORS

If Joe Biden manages to steal the White House, he has promised to amnesty tens of millions of illegal aliens. He will also likely amnesty the tens of thousands of blacks and antifa who have been rioting, looting, burning, and trashing America's cities.

"Amnesty" has the same root as "amnesia." It is a policy of forgetting about crimes and their victims and forgiving the perpetrators. The basic rationale of an amnesty is that although it allows criminals to get away with injustices, it benefits society as a whole because it allows us to put a traumatic episode like a civil war behind us rather than to let it drag on through legal recriminations.

The irony of amnestying black and antifa rioters is rather rich. BLM's main demand is to allow blacks to get away with crimes *today* because of crimes committed against blacks *centuries ago*. Those crimes, it seems, can never be forgiven or forgotten. But when it comes to looting shoe stores, torching businesses, and toppling monuments in the present day: perhaps we should forgive and forget. After all, we have to live with these people somehow. So maybe we should put the past behind us and look toward a future of "healing" and "unity."

Of course amnesty is a two-way street, and the Left will never forgive and forget about white crimes. Why abandon a good grift? Demanding recompense for "historical injustices" is a moral swindle in which blacks who have suffered no wrong demand apologies and benefits from whites who have not wronged them—all because *other* whites wronged *other* blacks, even centuries in the past.

Of course blacks are not held collectively responsible even for the crimes committed by other blacks in the present day. That would be condemned as a moral outrage. But if blacks who are alive today bear no guilt for the crimes of their contemporaries, then why do whites alive today bear guilt for the crimes of whites in centuries past?

Jonathan Bowden was famous for advising whites to simply "step over" the real and alleged historical crimes of our ancestors when our enemies throw them down in our path.[1] Slavery? I've stepped over it. Colonialism? I've stepped over it. The Holocaust? I've stepped over it.

Stepping over the past doesn't mean denying the facts of history. Nor does it require disputing whatever value judgments attach to those facts. It is simply a refusal to be bound by the past. I don't deny that slavery was real. I don't deny that it was immoral. I don't deny that there are lessons we can learn from it. But I am not morally obligated to suffer for it. I refuse to be swindled out of a future because of the crimes committed by white people in the past. It's that simple.

The concept of amnesty gives a legal basis for stepping over the past. A good example is the Indemnity and Oblivion Act of 1660 passed by the English Parliament after the restoration of the monarchy. The indemnity portion of the act was a general pardon for crimes committed during the Civil War and Interregnum, with certain unforgivable exceptions, such as the regicide of Charles I as well as piracy, buggery, rape, witchcraft, and murder (without government license). The oblivion portion of the act consigned the Interregnum to legal oblivion, meaning that it was illegal to discuss the crimes committed during that time. In short, forgive and forget—or else.

---

[1] Jonathan Bowden, "Credo: A Nietzschean Testament," *Western Civilization Bites Back*, ed. Greg Johnson (San Francisco: Counter-Currents, 2014).

What was the rationale for this act? The Civil War and Interregnum were worse than any individual crimes that occurred during them. Pursuing legal recourse for these crimes threatened the peace. Thus it was judged better to forgive and forget rather than risk the return of civil war.

The next time the Left demands that white people efface our past and surrender our future due to "historical crimes," just tell them you have amnestied your ancestors. We must also insist that respecting that amnesty is a non-negotiable condition for any future relations with non-whites. We need to end the swindle now, so future generations of white people will think us worthy of thanking and remembering, not forgiving and forgetting.

Counter-Currents, November 11, 2020

The 2018 Midterm Elections:
A Near-Death Experience?

The 2018 US midterm elections were actually very good for Donald Trump. As of this writing, the Republicans gained 3 seats in the Senate and lost 28 in the House of Representatives.

The Lying Press and certain White Nationalist commentators are, of course, spinning this as a repudiation of Trump. But that is false. It is a long-standing phenomenon in American politics that the party of sitting presidents loses in the midterm elections. Thus the yardstick to measure with is what happened in past midterm elections.

In the 1994 midterm elections, Bill Clinton's party lost 8 seats in the Senate and 54 seats in the House. In the 2010 midterm elections, Barack Obama's party lost 6 seats in the Senate and 63 seats in the House.

The worst-case scenario was a Democratic takeover of both houses, which would have allowed Trump's impeachment. Republicans lost seats in the House of Representatives but gained in the Senate. If the House votes to impeach Trump, the Senate will stop them. Democratic control of the House will, however, stop more standard Stupid Party tax cuts, which is a good thing, for it will help Trump re-focus on what got him elected in the first place: border security, economic nationalism, and an America First foreign policy.

There is every sign that Trump is refocusing on these essentials. For in the last weeks of the campaign, Trump seems to have had a political near-death experience. He saw just how perilous his hold on power really is. He saw just how suicidally stupid Republican politicians are, running on tax cuts and economic growth while America is disappearing before our very eyes. He saw the migrant caravans being formed and sped toward the border for a *Camp of the Saints* test of nerve. He saw Jews weaponizing the Pittsburgh synagogue massacre against him and the First Amendment. He saw Jews in the *Forward* and the *New York Times* openly admit that anti-white race-replacement immigration is regarded as a path to permanent power by the Jewish community and the Democratic Party.[1]

The Left decided to make this election a referendum on Donald Trump. Fortunately, Trump is far more popular than most Republicans. So Trump sprang into action, with a frenzied and grueling schedule of campaign rallies that would have killed many younger, weaker men. For a few weeks, we saw the Trump we loved from the 2015–2016 campaign again. Whatever happened to that guy? We want him back.

Well, it worked. Based on past midterm elections, this could have been much, much worse. Trump may have just saved his presidency. It remains to be seen if he has just saved America.

In truth, the losses were well-deserved. The Republicans deserved to lose because they strayed from Trump's populism. Trump deserved to lose, because he strayed from his populism too. By returning to basics at the last possible moment, he almost performed a midterm miracle. Again, it could have been so much worse.

But a lot of us are skeptical now. We are wondering if Trump trotted out ending birthright citizenship and other populist red meat merely to save himself and his worthless party for another round of tax cuts, foreign policy distractions, and fundamental betrayals of white America.

---

[1] Peter Beinart, "The Special Kind of Hate That Drove Pittsburgh Shooter—And Trump," *Forward*, October 28, 2018. Michelle Goldberg, "We Can Replace Them," *New York Times*, October 29, 2018.

Trump has to start delivering, or we will not fall for the same routine in 2020.

A near-death experience is often an occasion to examine one's life. When one actually feels in one's guts just how short and contingent life can be, one tends to re-evaluate one's priorities. One gives more time to genuinely important things. One lets the small stuff slide. Trump saw his whole presidency flashing before his eyes. Let's hope he saw much more: America's death or rebirth. Let's hope that he gets back to Making America Great Again.

This election was also a near-death experience for the Right, especially White Nationalists. We should know by now that we can't depend upon Republicans, and Trump himself is at best on probation. We can only depend on ourselves.

We've got to stop deluding ourselves with white pills and powders. We were never the vanguard of Trumpian populism. Nor is our job to delude others with Trumpian 4D chess apologetics.

From the very start of Trump's campaign, I said that White Nationalists need to use Trump, rather than let Trump use us. When Trump was first elected, I said that White Nationalists need to play the role of Trump's loyal opposition on the Right.

We want him to succeed. But he won't succeed unless we constantly battle against the bad policies and people who have deflected his administration for the first two years from the national populist vision that got him elected. Our greatest assets are truth and the credibility that comes from speaking it. Some of us have squandered that capital shamelessly for the past two years.

Trump is not the last chance for the white race in North America. He is merely the last chance to save the present American system. He is *their* last chance, not *ours*. But the establishment is too stupid to realize that, so they want him gone. A lot of them want him dead. By opposing him, they only hasten their own end.

White Nationalists need to get serious again. Trump will probably not save us. That was always a long shot. Thus we have to save ourselves. We would be flattering ourselves to claim that *we* are the last hope for the white race in North America, since many generations to come will join this battle. But we should act *as if* that is true. We should weigh our every word, our every deed, as if the fate of the world is entirely on our shoulders. It focuses the mind wonderfully.

White Nationalists have been drifting from defeat to defeat since Trump's victory. We were strongest when we were a leaderless, non-hierarchical, largely online metapolitical movement attacking the false ideas and terrible consequences of multiculturalism, as well as mocking the stupidity and moral squalor of the establishment.

We became weaker when we decided prematurely that it was time to follow leaders into street confrontations with antifa and the political system that coddles them. We can win any argument or flame war. But we can't win street battles. It is time for us to get back to what works: metapolitics, the propaganda war. For all the bluff posturing about taking the streets, we do not control one square inch of American territory. But once we change minds, the establishment has proven itself powerless to change them back.

Counter-Currents, November 8, 2018

WHY WHITE NATIONALISTS LIKE ANDREW YANG

The following text is an interview I gave to a reporter. I don't know if it will be used, but I made it clear that I would publish the full text at *Counter-Currents*. Now the whole world can quote from it.

White Nationalists need to understand exactly why I think Andrew Yang is important. As far as I am concerned, nothing essential depends on whether he is sincere about his proposals, gets the Democratic nomination, wins the presidency, or can implement his policies—even though I would like all those things to be true. If your first instinct is to splutter out any of those objections, you don't understand what I am doing here and why such considerations are irrelevant.

I can't control any of those factors, and neither can any other White Nationalist. What we *can* do is use Yang as an occasion to inject ideas that are important to White Nationalists into broader popular discussions, which is what I am doing here. As always, the key is to use politicians, not let politicians use us.

1. What are your general thoughts about the Trump administration?
White Nationalists supported Trump because he supported some policies that we also favor, principally immigration restrictions (including the border wall and the Muslim ban), protectionism, and an America First foreign policy. We think these policies are objectively good for the white majority.

I have no doubt that Trump was sincere about these policies when he announced them. He could have won the

Republican nomination and the presidency without them. He chose to fight a two-front war against the Democrats and his own party because he thought these issues were important.

But once in the White House, Trump lacked the skills and—let's be frank—the character and the moral seriousness to keep his promises. The cucking started hot and heavy from the very beginning of his administration. I wrote my "God Emperor No More" essay on April 8, 2017 after the Syria strike.[1]

Trump spent his first two years giving Jews and Republicans whatever they wanted, without first getting what he wanted from them. I didn't need to read a book on *The Art of the Deal* to see how stupid that was.

I hoped that the midterm elections were a near-death experience that might have got Trump back on track. But no. We're still waiting for that executive order on birthright citizenship.

The last straw for most White Nationalists came in the 2019 State of the Union address, when the boomer-con in Trump came out with an *ad lib* on increasing immigration, as long as it is *legal*. Then he doubled down on it. "Illegal" immigration is a coward's and a cuck's—that is to say, a Republican's—way of talking about immigration, because it is a euphemism for the real problem: non-white immigration.

We need immigration restrictions because most immigrants—legal and illegal—are not white, and as their numbers grow, America will increasingly resemble the Third World countries from which they come. Trump actually referred to these countries as "shitholes."

But now he is claiming that "our corporations" need more immigrants from shithole countries because "It's

---

[1] Greg Johnson, "God Emperor No More," *Toward a New Nationalism* (San Francisco: Counter-Currents, 2019).

good for the economy." The populists who put Trump in office don't think the profits of corporations are a good reason to further wreck the ethnic composition and harmony of the nation. This is standard Republican talk. As soon as a lot of White Nationalists heard that, they were simply through.

It is not so much that White Nationalists are off the Trump train. The trouble is that Trump is off the Trump train. We didn't change. He did.

2. Do you feel that Trump has helped to make White Nationalist thought more mainstream?

Trump made the discussion of some of our issues more mainstream, and indirectly he opened the way to more mainstream discussion of our more fundamental ideas, if only because the Left wanted to stigmatize Trump by trotting out some of his more extreme supporters.

Even though Trump has been a disappointment as a President, he made important—and permanent—metapolitical gains.

First of all, he broke the Republican gentlemen's agreement to never broach populist measures like immigration restriction and protectionism.

Second, Trump helped reorient political debate in America away from the false and superficial opposition between Republicans and Democrats to the deeper issues of nationalism and populism versus globalism and elitism. The American people want a socially conservative interventionist state that protects the working and middle classes from globalist oligarchs. Trump offered that synthesis.

The other parties are united by their refusal to give the people what they want. Republicans pay lip service to conservative values. Democrats pay lip service to using the state to defend the people from elites, as well as to fewer wars. But in reality, both parties only deliver what the current oligarchy wants: global capitalism and foreign adventurism combined with ultra-Leftist values.

In the end, Trump gave the oligarchs what they want, too. But there will be a new champion of national populist values, because that is what the people want, they are increasingly aware of it, and they are increasingly convinced that they will only get it by sweeping away the current political establishment.

Third, Trump triggered the Left to drop the mask of sanity. I don't think the days of civility will ever return. White Americans are increasingly aware that the Left doesn't simply hate Trump. The Left hates them and their values and wishes to replace them with non-whites. Democracy involves different groups in society trading power. That is really possible only if the different groups regard their rivals as part of the same overall people. White Americans are increasingly aware that the Left is not "their people." It is a coalition of non-whites and alienated, atypical whites, united by hatred of the white majority.

There will come a time—perhaps in 2020, perhaps in 2024—when white Americans will not cede power to the Left, no matter what the outcome of the election. That means that American democracy is broken. The Democrats broke it. But Trump was the trigger.

3. Do those in the White Nationalist and far-Right movement feel that President Trump supports them, after recent comments claiming that the movement is small?

No serious White Nationalist was under the illusion that Trump supported us. He used to support ideas that we supported. But those ideas stopped far short of White Nationalism.

As for his comment that our movement is small and full of problems, that is indeed true. We have a lot of problematic people because American civilization is collapsing, and white men are the primary victims. We have lots of people who are alienated and unemployed. We have lots of people from broken homes, fractured by the drugs, alcohol, and drama of selfish and degenerate parents. We have lots of people with drug and alcohol problems and personality disorders of their own. We have lots of people who are willing to lash out violently against the system that has betrayed them.

We had rather hoped that President Trump might help these problem people, by tackling globalization, immigration, the opioid crisis, and other maladies afflicting white America. But he's turned his back on us.

However, as long as white dispossession continues—as long as whites see their communities declining because of diversity and their living standards destroyed by globalization and immigration, all to a din of anti-white hate coming from the mainstream media and academia—our numbers will only grow. White dispossession due to immigration and globalization is the primary force driving the rise of national populism in every white country. White Nationalists are not causing this wave. But we are going to surf it to power and influence.

The closer an election is, the more important small groups of people become—especially highly energetic, motivated, and creative groups. Our movement was even smaller in 2016, when we were Trump's most ardent supporters and the scourge of the cuckservatives. But we didn't just post memes and arguments. We also voted, encouraged other people to vote, and worked to counter voter fraud. Trump won by a razor-thin margin: 107,000 votes in Michigan, Wisconsin, and Pennsylvania. He knows very well how important our efforts were in the last forty-eight hours of the campaign to flip those states. He won't win again without us.

4. What are your thoughts on candidate Andrew Yang, and has there been a general shift from those

in the movement beginning to support him for President? If so, when did people first begin to support him, and how often do you encounter mentions of Yang online?

Andrew Yang seems like an intelligent and sincere guy. He is not white, but he is the only Democrat who opposes anti-white identity politics. He is also the only Democrat who has talked about the problems afflicting white America. I will vote for him in the Democratic primary, and I will vote for him as President if he goes up against Trump.

Yang appeared right around the time Trump announced his final betrayal on immigration. Many White Nationalists immediately shifted their support to him. Yang memes became omnipresent overnight. Generally speaking, those White Nationalists who fully embrace national populism immediately saw Yang's appeal. Those who still retain residual elements of mainstream conservatism—especially the ideology of "free market" economics—are skeptical of Yang. But they will come around in the end.

5. What are your thoughts on Yang's universal basic income proposal?

I have been an advocate of universal basic income (UBI), and more broadly Social Credit economics, since 2011. See my essay "Money for Nothing."[2] I have also been an advocate of debt repudiation. See "Thoughts on Debt Repudiation."[3]

A universal basic income is an excellent idea for several reasons.

First, it is a way of creating money and putting it in the

---

[2] Greg Johnson, "Money for Nothing," *Truth, Justice & a Nice White Country*.

[3] Greg Johnson, "Thoughts on Debt Repudiation," *Truth, Justice & a Nice White Country*.

hands of consumers that bypasses two vast and parasitic categories of middlemen: banks, which charge interest, and social welfare bureaucracies.

Second, it is a way of dealing with the consequences of automation. When automation puts people out of work, they can't be allowed to starve. Besides, somebody has to buy and use the products of machines. We can automate production, but not consumption. The whole point of the economy, after all, is to provide goods and services for *people*.

Third, it would be good for the arts and culture. It would free people from basic material necessity to pursue educational and creative activities.

The knee-jerk reaction of those schooled in the ideological pseudo-science of "free market" economics, namely that a UBI would cause "inflation" is highly dubious. (See my essay "The Austrian Economic Apocalypse?"[4])

To make a UBI work, however, we would have to make some important changes in our present society.

First, the best way to fund a UBI is not to raise the money by taxes or borrowing, but for the state simply to create money out of nothing. We need to move to a pure fiat currency that is entirely decommoditized, i.e., a currency no longer subject to interest, inflation, or deflation—perhaps even a currency that cannot be saved.

Second, the UBI should not just be a safety net for people put out of work by mechanization. The overriding goal of public policy should be to promote scientific and technological advancement *to put us all out of work*. Our aim should be the *Star Trek* economy, in which material scarcity has been abolished by technology. See my essay "Technological Utopianism and Ethnic Nationalism."[5]

---

[4] Greg Johnson, "The Austrian Economic Apocaplyse," *Truth, Justice & a Nice White Country*.

[5] Greg Johnson, "Technological Utopianism and Ethnic Na-

Third, creating a UBI would necessitate limits to immigration, both legal and illegal. We cannot give a UBI to the entire planet. Our country is already being flooded by people looking for free stuff.

Fourth, a society with a UBI will have to create conditions in which leisure promotes self-cultivation, not self-destruction. It would have to address the problem of highly addictive and destructive habits—not just alcohol and drugs, but also pornography and videogaming—otherwise a UBI will simply enable large numbers of people to waste their lives. We will also have to give people more positive things to do with their leisure by improving education, giving subsidies to edifying forms of high culture, and encouraging public spiritedness over private hedonism.

6. Are White Nationalists legitimately supporting Yang, or is this just rhetoric online on sites like Gab and 4chan?

I think that quite a few White Nationalists sincerely support Yang because he has better policies for whites than anyone else in the race. Others support him just as a protest, because they are heartily sick of Trump. If America is going to hell, they figure, why not have America going to hell plus a thousand dollars a month? Others are just enjoying the Yang memes and the new sense of excitement, purpose, and unity Yang has brought us.

7. For those who do support Yang, how do they respond to his statements that he rejects support from White Nationalists?

Of course he rejects our support. Yang is probably sincerely anti-racist, while we would prefer to live in a society in which there are no Andrew Yangs at all. But generally speaking, White Nationalists find Asians to be the most

---

tionalism," *Toward a New Nationalism.*

agreeable non-white group in our society. This is a movement full of anime fanatics, with a fringe of rice burners. Many of them would welcome our new Asian overlord.

Beyond that, we are genuinely pragmatic. We supported Trump despite his obvious faults, because he coincided with our interests. Now that Yang looks like he will advance our interests, we're Democrats. Now the Democrats really are "the real racists."

Yang might not like us. But here's the thing. He will still cash our checks, and he can't prevent us from arguing for the merits of his proposals, voting for him, and encouraging others to vote for him. Whether he likes it or not, White Nationalists might put him in the White House.

8. Are those in the White Nationalist and far-Right movement feeling more emboldened than ever before?

In a word, yes.

Long-term demographic trends are ominous. As I argue in *The White Nationalist Manifesto*,[6] if we do nothing—if we do not implement White Nationalist policies—the white race will go extinct. That concentrates the mind wonderfully. That imparts urgency and moral seriousness to our cause. But white extinction is still a couple centuries away. So we also have some time to maneuver and turn things around.

Moreover, medium-term demographic and political trends are working in our favor. As Roger Eatwell and Matthew Goodwin argue in *National Populism: The Revolt Against Liberal Democracy*,[7] the rise of national populism

---

[6] Greg Johnson, "White Extinction" and "White Genocide," *The White Nationalist Manifesto*.

[7] Greg Johnson, "National Populism Is Here to Stay," *White Identity Politics*.

is being fueled by four deep-seated trends that are not going to abate any time soon: distrust of the establishment, destruction of communities by immigration, the decline of white working-class and middle-class living standards due to globalization, and the breakdown of people's alignments with existing political parties.

Eatwell and Goodwin actually argue that the only way we will get beyond national populism is if established parties adopt national populist policies. Which means that the days of globalist hegemony are over, and the future belongs to competing forms of national populism. That is an environment in which White Nationalists will flourish.

The primary cause of rising white racial consciousness is *not* White Nationalists like me. Instead, people are waking up in response to objective events—because diversity causes conflict and globalization causes deprivation. Once people wake up, White Nationalists try to deepen their understanding of why these processes are taking place and offer workable political alternatives. But even if we were completely censored and deplatformed, racial polarization and social breakdown will continue to rise until we abandon multiculturalism and globalization and adopt national populist ideas.

White Nationalists win every honest debate, because truth is on our side. Censorship and deplatforming won't stop us, because to do that, you'd have to shut down the internet, and the global economy depends upon it. Immigration and globalization are pushing more people in our direction all the time, and the establishment keeps doubling down on the same failed policies. And now, with the rise of Andrew Yang, American White Nationalists have a new cause around which to unite our warring tribes. White Nationalists have good reason to feel more emboldened than ever.

Counter-Currents, March 25, 2019

The Iran Opportunity

I'd like to say that the assassination of Qasem Soleimani isn't the end of the world, but it's too soon to say, because world wars have started with similar provocations.

It is, however, safe to say that Donald Trump has made his dumbest foreign policy decision yet, for the same reason he made all of his other dumb foreign policy decisions: listening to the Israel First lobby ("neocons") who basically control the Republican Party when it comes to foreign policy.

Assassinating a foreign general is an act of war. It doesn't matter if Trump denies that. It doesn't matter if he says it ends here. That is not in his hands. Whether it ends here is now in the hands of Iran, and the Iranians say they want revenge. If Iran—or its proxies, or its allies, or independent sympathizers, or even Israelis acting under a false flag—assassinate an American general or carry out a terrorist attack on American soil, then the US will retaliate. Trump has already promised to destroy Iranian targets, including—taking a page from the Taliban and ISIS—important cultural sites.

The stupidity of risking war with Iran was made crystal clear by the announcement on December 30, 2019, of a Taliban cease-fire in Afghanistan as a prelude to signing a peace treaty with the United States. The Taliban is an Islamic political movement that ruled Afghanistan from 1998 to 2001, when the US overthrew them. George W. Bush was told it would be a "cakewalk" and that Americans would be "greeted as liberators." But the Taliban smoothly transitioned from ruling government to guerilla insurgency. And 18 years later—after more than three thousand US coalition deaths, uncounted injuries, uncounted Afghan deaths and injuries, and billions of dollars in expenditures—a few thousand medieval fanatics have fought the United States to a draw, and we are now contemplating a peace agreement with them. (Because negotiating with terrorists is something that we do all the time.)

The same people who sold George W. Bush on the idea that the wars in Afghanistan and Iraq would be cakewalks are steering Donald Trump toward a war with Iran. Iran has a mountainous terrain similar to neighboring Afghanistan. But the similarities end there. Iran is a nation of 82 million people. It has a huge standing army with high-tech weapons, which the Russians and Chinese are eager to resupply. Iran has allies all over the Muslim world and beyond. There is also an Iranian diaspora in Europe and the United States (two million in the US alone), some of whom are Iranian government assets and many more of whom would side with Iran if the US started attacking their cousins. Does the United States—a nation that is now politically divided about even having a border—have the political will to intern two million Iranians?

Beyond that, when the US attacked Afghanistan and Iraq, it enjoyed a great deal of international sympathy due to the 9/11 terrorist attacks. That good will has been spent. Moreover, the US was united behind George W. Bush. Trump is a highly polarizing figure, at home and abroad. He simply does not have the political capital to start a war, unless he wants to sacrifice his reelection bid and his place in history to the Moloch in Jerusalem. (He might.)

America is a much weaker country today than in 2001, in large part because of the wars in Afghanistan and Iraq. A war in Iran might be the last straw. This could be the end of the American Empire, and there is reason to wonder if the regime at home could survive the collapse of its empire.

In the eyes of people all over the globe, Trump's assassination of Soleimani makes America look weak rather than strong. That's why Iraq's parliament has voted to expel the US from its soil. As soon as the US is overextended in Iran, expect terrorism, revolutions, coups, and insurgencies in every outpost of the American Empire.

So, at the very least, we can say that *an American war against Iran would have a much worse outcome for America than our war in Afghanistan.*

But we all knew that something like this could happen from the very start of Trump's candidacy. Despite his promises of an America First foreign policy, Trump parroted the worst neocon talking points about Iran. I still supported Trump, however, because on balance the rest of his policies were good—some of them decisive breaks with Republican orthodoxy. Beyond that, the alternative was Hillary Clinton.

I take solace in the fact that the pain we are feeling at every new blustering tweet—the embarrassment, the cringe that reaches to our very core, continuing on into the subatomic level—must be what Leftists are feeling *every single day.*

So what should White Nationalists do about this horrible blunder?

First, we should take stock: there are some things we can do, and some things that we can't.

We have a shrinking number of beleaguered outposts on the internet from which we can speak the truths that the establishment denies. Despite all the attempts to deplatform us, our audience and our credibility are growing. This is where we need to concentrate our efforts. No matter what Trump's blunder leads to, we can turn it to our advantage by using it as an opportunity to speak forbidden truths.

In this case, the most target-rich environment is on the Right. Soleimani's assassination is a great opportunity to educate our people about:

- Jewish influence on American foreign policy: how the preferences of more than sixty million Americans who voted for an America First foreign policy were canceled by a few Jewish billionaires like Sheldon Adelson who want Israel to always come first
- The bloody-minded stupidity of Republicans who are cheering on the most reckless foreign adventure of the last fifty years
- The bloody-minded stupidity of the Republican grifters who have taken over the MAGA movement and made it indistinguishable from the neocons who brought us the disasters in Afghanistan and Iraq
- The truth about people who might be mistaken for our allies but who are now taking positions indistinguishable from neocons, e.g., Nick Fuentes, Curt Doolittle, Anne Marie Waters, Katie Hopkins, and Tommy Robinson

We will never have a genuine national populist movement and an America First foreign policy until we clean house of the people who have polluted the American Right with neocon talking points, bellicose delusions about American exceptionalism, and the idea that America's status as the vanguard of liberal degeneracy gives it the right to force it on the rest of the world at gunpoint.

For the most part, our forces are doing a very good job so far, but I have three caveats.

- We lack the numbers, money, or legitimacy to constitute a voting bloc, so pretending that we are going to punish Trump by throwing the election to the Democrats just makes us sound like hysterical fantasists, which undermines the credibility that is one of our biggest assets.

❖ Right now, the United States is in the intolerable position of being merely a plaything of Jewish interests. It is a failure to take our own side, however, if we simply reflexively take the side of our enemy's enemies.
❖ Suggesting that we should put the likes of Elizabeth Warren in the White House because of Iran is tantamount to saying that we would hasten to destroy America because we suddenly identify with a Muslim nation—or, what is closer to the truth: that we hate Israel more than we love ourselves.

While the rest of the world loses its head about the new Iran Crisis, we need to keep calm and exploit this golden Iran Opportunity.

Counter-Currents, January 7, 2020

WIGNATS WHIRR FOR WAR

Four years ago, when Donald Trump glided down the golden escalator at Trump Tower and declared his candidacy for President of the United States, he broke the Republican gentleman's agreement never to talk about the negative consequences of immigration and globalization.

Trump's America First, national populist stances on immigration, globalization, and foreign policy resonated with millions of Americans: Republicans, independents, and even Democrats. Enough to win him the nomination and the Presidency.

But, as I never tire of pointing out, Trump did not have to take these positions to win. The whole system is premised on not giving the people what they want. Trump could have played by the system's rules. Trump could have xeroxed the Jeb! platform and still won, based simply on his celebrity, money, and personality. In fact, it would have been easier for Trump to win that way, because by running a national populist campaign, he had to fight a two-front war against Hillary Clinton and the Republican Party/Conservative Inc. establishment.

When a man pays a huge price to campaign on issues that he didn't need to win, that tells me that he is sincere. That's why I believed Trump could save America. That's why I did everything in my power to get him elected.

So what happened to the Trump presidency? Obviously, Trump encountered forces stronger than his convictions about what is necessary to save America. Many of these forces are external. Blackmail cannot be ruled out. Historians will be puzzling out the enigma of Trump well into the next century.

But whatever forces were brought to bear, in the end Trump had to *decide* to go along with them. He went along with the Republican donor class. He went along with the Jewish lobby. He had a chance to save America, but instead he chose to go along with the parasites that are killing it. Trump ultimately allowed himself to be swallowed by the swamp.

Donald Trump is a tragic figure in the true sense of the word. We are witnessing the terrifying spectacle of a man of genuine greatness failing because of his own grievous faults. Vanity is clearly one of them, including a willingness to settle for appearances rather than substance. Lack of moral seriousness is another. But probably the worst is anti-intellectualism, which led him to adopt principles that are incompatible with America's survival and his own better instincts. Principles like the civic nationalist creedal conception of American identity, or the idiotic notion that America would be enriched by jihadis, MS-13 members, and millions upon millions of Shitholians, if only they came here *legally*.

The tragedy of Trump is also the tragedy of America: the downfall of a genuinely great nation because of its own fatal flaws. I fear that there are not enough serious men left in America to save her.

But this is not about Trump the man. It was never about Trump the man. It was always about using Trump to get our ideas in circulation and open the minds of our people. Great minds discuss ideas. Average minds discuss events. Small minds discuss people.

Trump was not the last chance for white people in North America. But he was the last chance to salvage the United States of America, from sea to shining sea. For more than half a century, the Left has been scheming to create a one-party Democratic dictatorship by flooding the country with black and brown people, who vote disproportionately for Democrats.

Third World immigration is election tampering.

If Trump had built the wall, deported millions of illegal aliens, eliminated systematic Democratic voter fraud, and reversed white demographic decline, he could have saved America as a prosperous, First World country. He could also have saved the American system of two-party democracy.

But Trump failed. Trump will be the last Republican President. And he will be a one-term President. Already, there are probably not enough sane white people in America to reelect him. What comes next is a Democratic one-party state that will resemble Mexico: a violent, corrupt, squalid, and socialistic non-white society ruled by a tiny white and Jewish elite of ultra-rich sociopaths mouthing Left-wing slogans.

Imagine a Beto stamping on a brown face, forever.

There is, however, still a chance to avoid that. It is a slim chance. But it is worth taking. White Nationalists could rally the nearly sixty million people who voted for Trump in 2016 and begin the process of creating a homeland for whites in North America.

Only a few people learn from history. Even fewer learn from reason. Most people learn only from experience, and the most vivid lessons come from suffering. White Nationalists have been warning our people for years that our livelihoods, our nation, and our future are being stolen from us through race replacement immigration, which not only reduces wages and wrecks communities but is also a form of demographic gerrymandering.

Demographic displacement invalidates democracy. The whole point of democracy is to make the elites serve the interests of the people. If the elites fail the people, the people dissolve the government and elect a new one that will faithfully serve their interests.

Democracy becomes a sham when elites conspire to stay in power by rigging elections. One form of election-rigging is to stuff ballot boxes with fake votes. Another form is to register people who are not qualified to vote, including dead people and non-citizens. (It is tragic that many people will vote Republican their whole lives, then die and become Democrats.)

But the most insidious form of election tampering is for the government to dissolve the people and elect a new one through demographic replacement.

On election night, 2020, sixty million white Americans are going to finally *experience* what we have been warning them about for decades. They are going to *see* their country stolen from them through non-white immigration. They are going to *see* the beginning of the Democratic one-party dictatorship.

But when America becomes a banana republic, and democracy becomes an obvious sham, then why should white Americans abide by the results? Why should they allow their nation to be stolen from them? Why shouldn't they take it back?

Now I have a serious question to pose to White Nationalists: If you want our movement to be in a position to mobilize the Trump electorate and turn it into a genuinely revolutionary national populist movement, what should our stance be today and going into the 2020 election?

Should we openly declare war on "Blompf"? Should we pour scorn on the "boomers" and "normies" who still support him? Should we announce our intention to tip the 2020 election to the Democrats?

Believe me, folks, I understand the temptation. The ASAP Rocky fiasco is surely one of the most surreal and undignified episodes in the history of the American Presidency. I understand why the Left would like to exploit the El Paso massacre to grab power, but it boggles the mind that Trump and the Republicans are basically willing to *throw power away*, undermining the First and Second Amendments merely to appease raving lunatics who think anyone to the Right of Hillary Clinton should be censored, disarmed, and eventually replaced by brown helots.

But how, exactly, would declaring war on Blompf qualify us to rally the dejected and disillusioned Trump electorate? Wouldn't they simply regard us as their enemies, who collaborated in their dispossession? Wouldn't they be *right* to do so?

The term "wignat" is short for "wigger nationalist." A wigger is a white person who acts like a black. A wigger nationalist is a White Nationalist who acts like a black, specifically someone with dumb ideas and high time preferences. There's no need to name names. It is a term of abuse, meant to draw blood. The wignats have now declared war on President Trump.[1] I think this is dumb and self-defeating.

The wignats met their Waterloo in Charlottesville and the subsequent "optics wars." Their organizations have collapsed, and they are trying to rehabilitate themselves on YouTube, Twitter, and various blogs by competing to issue the most strident and embittered denunciations of Donald Trump and the American nationalists who trounced them in the optics wars.

But wignat self-indulgence gets us nowhere.

What should White Nationalists do about Trump? First of all, we need to understand the battle we are in.

- ❖ We're the good guys, the national populists who represent the interests of white Americans.
- ❖ The bad guys are the political establishment, including the Republican Party and Conservatism Inc. (I support total war against these people.)
- ❖ The people we are trying to win over are the sixty million people who voted for Donald Trump, many of whom fervently support him.

To win their support, we cannot simply lump Trump

---

[1] Hunter Wallace, "White Nationalists Should Declare War on Conservatism," *Occidental Dissent*, August 6, 2019.

with the political establishment. For one thing, it isn't true. He is still at odds with the establishment, and when he gets back on the campaign trail, he will provide us with new opportunities to reach and radicalize the electorate. Thus we should treat Trump as still in play, because his electorate is very much in play.

We should praise Trump when he says something good. We should defend Trump when he is attacked unfairly. And we should criticize Trump when he does something dumb, especially when it provides us an opportunity to hammer home a more consistent national populist message.

When we criticize Trump, however, it is best to make it clear that all of his errors come from listening to the establishment rather than to the people and to his own political instincts. Given everything Trump has done for us in overturning the Republican consensus on nationalism and populism, I think we at least owe him the courtesy of holding out hope that somewhere, deep inside, he is still better than the establishment he is now slow-dancing with.

If we take this course, Trump voters will increasingly trust White Nationalists as the people who best articulate the national populist vision they hold in their hearts. That will put us in the position to take up the national populist standard when Trump goes down to defeat. But to win this game, we have to be in play as well.

If we take the wignat course, however, the Trump electorate will simply regard us as immature, petulant, self-marginalizing Never Trumpers who openly advocate handing the nation over to Elizabeth Warren or Kamala Harris. Once we have dug ourselves into that hole, how exactly are we going to connect with the people we need to lead?

The wignat war on Trump is as tactically stupid as the wignat war on American nationalism. Indeed, it is just another version of the same error. As I put it in my article "What is American Nationalism?":

> American White Nationalism is far more likely to win the battle for a white homeland than anti-American forms of White Nationalism. The white Americans who lean toward white identity politics, even implicitly, overwhelmingly vote for the Republican Party. They also tend to be conservative and patriotic. They identify with America and feel a strong attachment to American symbols.
>
> Like everyone else in our society, they have been miseducated about America's nature and history and think it was founded as a color-blind propositional nation.
>
> But they are also increasingly aware of the catastrophic consequences of diversity. Thus as white demographic displacement accelerates, these Americans will become increasingly receptive to our account of America's real identity, how our country has been hijacked by hostile aliens, and how we can Make America White Again.
>
> By contrast, anti-American White Nationalists will have to convince our people of all the same facts about race, diversity, and demographic displacement. But, as if that were not already enough of an uphill battle, they will also have to sell Americans a raft of anti-American ideas: cranky conspiracy theories about Freemasons, Southern Nationalism, and the like. The anti-Americans will also have to convince Americans of a whole host of historical revisionist theses about the Civil War, the Third Reich, and the Holocaust, none of them really necessary for white survival in America. Finally, the anti-Americans will have to explain away their use of symbols which are at best alien to Americans and at

worst are freighted with highly negative connotations.

Both forms of White Nationalism communicate the same truths. But American nationalists relate them to ideas that feel authentic to our target audience, while anti-American nationalists link them to ideas that at best strike most Americans as alien and inauthentic and at worse seem downright repugnant.

Which approach is likely to make more converts? Which approach is more likely to save the white race in America, which is really the only thing that matters? Clearly, anti-American White Nationalism is self-marginalizing and self-defeating. American nationalism is the only way forward.[2]

The inevitable wignat answer is that embracing American nationalism and refusing to alienate the Trump electorate is merely inauthentic pandering to "normies," whereas they are authentic and only speak the truth. Of course this is sheer pretense. Every wignat disaster from Hailgate to Charlottesville springs from pandering to—or embracing—the false premise that the only authentic form of national populism is neo-Nazism. But being a neo-Nazi in America today is not authentic. It is totally fake. It is a symptom of rootlessness and alienation, not a solution to them. So the real choice here is pandering to sixty million normal people—or a cringe-inducing fringe of freaks.

I have no doubt that Trump will lose in 2020. In fact, I think he will lose with or without the wignats. So I have a message to the wignats: You are powerless to affect the outcome of the election one way or another. But some-

---

[2] Greg Johnson, "What Is American Nationalism?," *Toward a New Nationalism*.

thing is in your power: There are talented polemicists and propagandists among you. You can change minds. You can either help build up White Nationalists as the natural leaders of American national populism after Trump—or you can continue down the road toward irrelevance. Choose wisely.

Counter-Currents, August 8, 2019

The 2020 US Presidential Race So Far

For decades now, White Nationalists have been telling Republicans that unless they halt the demographic decline of white America, their party is doomed, and the Democrats will create a one-party state.

There will come a time when all the Republican conventional wisdom—which, after all, is based on elections in a predominantly white America—will simply no longer be true. There will come a time when "The economy's good" will no longer save Republicans.

Indeed, in 2016, it was probably already impossible for a conventional Republican to get elected President. But then an unconventional Republican, Donald Trump, came along.

Trump's America First trade and foreign policies, and his promise to reduce immigration—most of which is non-white—spoke to the demographic anxieties of white Americans. Trump ran as a populist, not a Republican. He won the votes of blue-collar Democrats whose livelihoods are threatened by globalization. But, as a number of political scientists have argued since the election, economic populism was not enough to put Trump in the White House. His decisive advantage came from his appeal to white identity politics.

Even so, Trump won by a very narrow margin. Over the last four years, that margin has been shrinking as a lot of white Trump voters have died, while a lot of non-whites, who vote Democrat 70% of the time, have been added to the voter rolls.

To ensure his re-election, Trump needed to prioritize two things from his first day in office: (1) *stopping non-white immigration*, legal and illegal, and (2) *ending voter fraud*, which almost entirely committed by Democrats and their allies.

Indeed, non-white immigration is simply another form of election tampering. Just as Republican votes are negated by entering fake Democratic votes, or just changing vote tallies, when non-white immigrants are added to voter rolls, white Republican votes are negated. This is why the Left so eagerly promotes non-white immigration, both legal and illegal. The Left seeks to create a one-party state by demographically replacing white majorities with non-whites.

The Left's strategy makes a mockery of democracy. The democratic idea is that the government is more likely to secure the common good if the ruling elites are chosen by the people. It completely turns democratic legitimacy on its head if elites instead get to choose the people through race-replacement immigration schemes.

Mass immigration delegitimizes democracy.

The people are supposed to elect the government. The government is not supposed to elect the people. When elites engineer race-replacement immigration to maintain elite power, that is not democracy. That is the rule of the few, for their own interests, not the common good.

Trump has done some good things to reduce immigration and other forms of election tampering, but it was probably too little, too late. This means that the 2020 US Presidential Election is the Democrats' to lose.

But it looks like the Democrats may be just stupid enough to lose it.

Until this week, the frontrunner for the Democratic nomination was Senator Bernie Sanders of Vermont. Not only is Sanders a Marxist, and thus well to the Left of the Democratic mainstream, he is not even a member of the Democratic Party. Sanders is widely despised by the Democratic leadership, who reject Marxism for neoliberalism and non-white identity politics.

I didn't think Bernie's lead would last very long. After all, the Democrats are responsible for virtually all election fraud in America. They diddled Sanders out of the nomination in 2016, and they were prepared to do it again if they could not beat him any other way.

The only question in my mind was who the Democrats' nominee would be. He or she would have to be a centrist, because the oligarchy wants to keep its riches. That would eliminate Elizabeth Warren. So the nominee would be Joe Biden, Pete Buttigieg, Amy Klobuchar, Tom Steyer, or Mike Bloomberg.

I honestly did not think that Joe Biden would get the nomination. Biden has always been a weirdo, and now he's an old, feeble, senile weirdo. Biden has a long history of truly creepy behavior with women and girls. He has a long history of clumsy and pathological dishonesty: plagiarizing other politicians and telling bizarre lies. He and his family are obviously corrupt. He's a shameless shill for the usurious Delaware-based credit card industry.

Of course scandals like these never stopped the Clintons.

But Joe Biden is obviously falling apart. Thus far in the race, we have seen his false teeth come lurching out of his mouth, and we have seen one of his eyeballs fill up with blood.

Of course physical ailments never stopped Hillary Clinton.

But Joe Biden is obviously going senile. He is often visibly confused. He babbles incoherently. He mistakes his sister for his wife. He forgets what state he is in. He forgets what office he is running for. And, as he slips deeper into senility, his already wobbly self-control is getting ever weaker. Thus his creeping gets creepier, and his lies get weirder.

It is only going to get worse. As he moves from the primaries to the convention to the actual Presidential race, the punishing schedule and crushing stress will intensify. This drooling dolt should be staring vacantly at a TV in the geriatric wing of a prison, not running for President, much less actually being the President.

Many perceptive Democrats saw this, which is why Pete Buttigieg and Amy Klobuchar performed so well in the early primaries. I figured that if Buttigieg stayed in the race long enough for Biden and Sanders to fade, he could walk away with the nomination. He would be perfect for the Democrats. As a bland centrist, he would allow the oligarchy to continue raping the people, and as a gay historic first, he would allow them to feel good about themselves.

But then came the South Carolina primary, which is determined by (ahem) less perceptive Democrats. For some reason, African American voters don't see Biden's increasingly obvious cognitive decline as a disqualification, if they see it at all. Bernie bros refer to Biden supporters as "low-information voters." To be more precise, Biden was carried to victory by low-IQ blacks. Biden is so popular among black voters that outright fraud was probably not even necessary. He won handily.

Then the party establishment put the word out: It is time to unify behind Biden. Phone calls and horse-trading started. Buttigieg and Klobuchar were the first to drop out, followed by billionaires Steyer and Bloomberg.

All these people know that Biden is not qualified to be President. If they felt the slightest twinge of duty toward their country, or even just their party, they would have stayed in the race. But they're all calculating sociopaths. They expect to be well-rewarded for their treason.

Perhaps the Vice-Presidential slot was dangled as an incentive. Given that Biden will be unable to govern, whoever becomes his Vice President will very likely end up running the country, along with a camarilla—or should I say cabal?—of unelected party insiders.

What I want to know is: Who are the geniuses who put the fix in for Biden? Surely, their names are a matter of public record. Who decided—from a population of more than 300 million people—that Joe Biden is the most qualified man to be the next President of the United States? Wouldn't you like to know their names, in order to hold them accountable?

Buoyed by the departure of his centrist rivals, Biden trounced Sanders in the primaries on Super Tuesday (or, as Biden called it, "Super Thursday"). He may even have won without fraud.

Biden is now the presumptive nominee, although Sanders has been strengthened going into the next primaries by Elizabeth Warren's departure from the race.

Running a manifestly senile man for President is a consummate act of cynicism. The Democrats are committing a massive fraud against the American people. It is a bait and switch, because Joe Biden cannot perform the job he is running for. Instead, that will be handled primarily by people who are *not elected*.

Hereditary monarchy is supposed to be bad because occasionally a degenerate or mental incompetent is foisted upon the populace. But in late-stage democracies, such people are actually elected. That is far worse.

The sad truth is that there might just be enough cynics, dupes, and "stop-Trump-at-any-cost" hysterics to put Joe Biden in the White House.

I hope that Trump can beat Biden.

It is a gift to Trump to be opposed by the one Democrat less articulate than he is. If I were Trump, I would run as conciliatory and centrist a campaign as possible, since a lot of Democrats are going to have serious doubts about #SenileJoe. I would also confer with experts on dementia, to come up with strategies to exploit Biden's weaknesses in debates. Dementia does not just affect memory but also self-control. It would be nice if we could get footage of unhinged rage along with all the babbling and confusion. It is cruel, but not as cruel as delivering the Presidency to Joe Biden and the people who pull his strings.

If Biden is the nominee, it would be foolish for Trump to underestimate him, precisely because Biden *cannot* be the brains running his campaign. The Democratic Party may have stupid, crazy, and evil aims, but they are clever, disciplined, and evil in pursuing them.

From a metapolitical point of view, the best outcome is an election fought over the issues of globalism vs. nationalism, since that is a battle White Nationalists cannot lose. If Sanders were the nominee, the race would be about capitalism vs. socialism, which is not a debate worth having. I don't want the Koch and Cato types to have any relevance whatsoever. With Biden as the nominee, however, chances are this race will be entirely about personalities, not principles. I just pray that Trump will dial back his pointless and disgusting pandering to blacks.

This race might not be the opportunity to educate the public that we enjoyed in 2016, but it is bound to be entertaining.

Counter-Currents, March 5, 2020

A Year of Decision

Future historians may look back at 2020 and declare it a pivotal year in history, like 1989, when communism began its collapse in Europe; or 1914, when Europe threw itself into the abyss; or 410, when Rome was sacked; or even the birth of Christ, somewhere around the year 1. The year 2020 may be the beginning of the end of multiculturalism—and the beginning of the beginning for ethnonationalism.

We need to do our best to make that happen. We can't just count on the impersonal biological and social forces that are destroying multiculturalism before our eyes. We have to put our shoulder to the wheel of time and push the process forward. We also need to steer it toward something better by offering a real alternative. So whenever you have an opportunity to redpill people about the ongoing violence and insanity, just keep repeating the mantras:

"We can't live with these people."

"We don't have to live like this."

And, most importantly:

"If white people had a country of our own, this would not be happening."

We don't have to live this way. We can separate. We need a racial divorce.

To get that racial divorce, we need to *increase racial polarization* and *force a decision* to solve the problem *permanently* by going our separate ways. Blacks and the Left are doing a great job of increasing polarization for us, although we need to keep adding fuel to the fire. Forcing a decision will be even harder because it goes against the grain of our current leadership and our political system as a whole.

Carl Schmitt, and before him the great Spanish reactionary Juan Donoso Cortés, recognized that an essential feature of liberal democracy is *the evasion of decisions*.[1] What is a decision? A decision is required when you have a choice between *mutually exclusive* options, meaning that you have to take *one or the other*. You can't choose both, and you can't just choose not to decide. A real decision is the *forced* choice between mutually exclusive options.

Liberals evade decision for two main reasons.

First, liberals are optimists. They think that the arc of history bends toward a world without conflicts and thus without politics and hard political decisions.

Second, liberals are afraid of power and everything that comes with it, especially *personal responsibility*.[2] Decision requires that *someone* be invested with the *final authority* to decide, as well as the *responsibility* to bear the consequences. Liberals, however, think that we can be ruled by laws, not men, and when decisions need to be made, they prefer to make them collectively, hence the endless talk. Or they create complex "checks and balances," which are simply a way of treating responsibility like a hot potato, to be handed off to someone else. Or, to change the metaphor, it is like a game of musical chairs, where the last man standing loses by having to make a decision and stick by it.

---

[1] Greg Johnson, "Notes on Schmitt's *Crisis* and Ours," *Counter-Currents*, July 10, 2020 and "Schmitt, Sovereignty, and the Deep State," *Counter-Currents*, August 12, 2014.

[2] Greg Johnson, "Gun Control and Personal Responsibility," *Counter-Currents*, January 16, 2013.

America has now suffered more than three months of anti-white rioting by blacks and communists. As the death toll mounts and economic costs soar into the billions, the country's leadership either supports the lawlessness or is afraid to do anything about it. They are afraid of the mob and afraid of the press. But they are more afraid of their own consciences, since they have accepted the fake moral absolute that nothing is worse than racism toward non-whites, especially blacks.

Election-year pandering to black voters is surely a huge part of it too. Thus America drifts deeper into crisis, held hostage to the whims of the stupidest, most violent, and most sociopathic element of the population.

Every time a black criminal encounters the police—and there is a never-ending supply of black criminals—we risk more riots. Furthermore, as the state backs off from enforcing laws against blacks, black criminals naturally respond to the opportunity by committing more crimes.

If you want to destroy a society, just make it a taboo to arrest black people. They'll do the rest.

Eventually, a decision will have to be made. But by then, the damage to the nation may be irreparable. Furthermore, by driving decision and responsibility out of the political process, liberals just create a situation where ultimate decisions are made by unaccountable people outside the political system entirely, i.e., our disproportionately Jewish oligarchy.

For the duration of the crisis, race-conscious whites must:

- ❖ Stay out of direct confrontations with blacks and communists. The establishment wishes to push the absurd lie that we are responsible for the violence. Don't give them any help doing that.
- ❖ Do everything we can, aside from direct con-

frontations, to heighten the tensions and present our workable ethnonationalist alternative: complete separation from blacks.
- ❖ Do everything we can to force a decision. A serious country would have crushed this insurrection long ago. The US *has* crushed such insurrections. But the underlying problem was allowed to remain. Blacks and whites cannot live in the same society. If Trump finally cracks down, normies will breathe a sigh of relief, and the problem will be allowed to fester until the next insurrection, when whites are an even smaller and weaker part of the population. The only solution is complete racial separation, and the more people who demand it—and the sooner—the better.

We also need to re-elect Donald Trump, not because of what Trump is likely to do, but because:

- ❖ Trump's reelection will heighten polarization even more.
- ❖ Trump will not strip whites of our First and Second Amendment rights, which will leave us freer to organize.
- ❖ Trump will not intervene to overturn national populist regimes in Europe.

Yes, it would have been nice to have gotten a wall.

Yes, it would have been nice if Trump had taken serious steps to combat electoral fraud and tech censorship.

Yes, it would have been nice if Trump had turned America in the right direction.

But that's up to us now. We can expect no help from anyone in power. Whites have no representation in Washington, no friends in office. Trump, however, will do less to impede us, and his very presence will polarize and delegitimize the system better than we ever could. Trump gives us more crises and more opportunities to triumph in the end. Four more years of Trump will get us closer to the ethnostate.

Counter-Currents, October 30, 2020

WIGNAT WHEXIT

In 2016, Donald Trump ran as a populist and won. In 2020, his bid for re-election followed the standard Republican playbook. There was a lot of talk about the stock market, very little populist talk about immigration, globalization, and protectionism. There was a good deal of conservative culture war rhetoric to mobilize patriots and evangelicals. Finally, there was a huge amount of pandering to blacks, Jews, Hispanics, Asians, and homosexuals: identity politics for everyone but whites. But Trump's white base—especially the white, working-class swing voters who put him over the top in the Midwest—were basically taken for granted.

For race-conscious whites, it was infuriating. Naturally, a lot of us decided that maybe we should sit this election out and show Trump that we are not going to be taken for granted. The Republicans are going to have to engage in white identity politics if they are to get white votes. Maybe if we tank Trump's reelection and deliver the Senate to the Democrats as well, they'll finally take us seriously. Time for a Whexit.

"Whexit" means "white exit." But I am speaking specifically of a Whexit of *racially-conscious whites*. This idea is being especially championed in wignat quarters of the movement. "Wignat" stands for "wigger nationalist" and refers to White Nationalists who are handicapped by low IQs and high time preferences. Of course not every White Nationalist who thinks this way is a wignat, but there's a strong correlation.

Is a White Nationalist Whexit going to work?

Probably not. First, such a Whexit is based on a false understanding of Republican motives. Second, it is based on a superficial understanding of human psychology. Finally, it is based on delusions about the size and power of the racially-conscious white community.

Why do Republicans pander to non-whites but scrupulously avoid addressing specifically white interests? The moral consensus in America today is that racism is the worst thing in the world, but only for white people. Republicans follow that code to the letter, hence they are willing to appeal to the identities and collective interests of Jews, blacks, and other groups, but they will never explicitly address the identity and interests of whites. In our case, the best we can hope for is that our identity and interests will be subsumed under the national interest or the rights of mankind as a whole.

Does this help the Republicans at the polls? Yes. Does it gain them minority votes? Probably a few, and in close races, even a shift of a fraction of a percent of non-white votes can put Republicans over the top.

But wouldn't Republicans gain even more votes if they followed the Sailer strategy and just focused on increasing their share of the white vote, perhaps by making explicit appeals to white identity politics?

The Republicans obviously think not. Why? The moral consensus in America today is that racism is the worst possible thing, but only for whites. Thus it is enormously important for one's reputation to demonstrate that one is not a racist. That is why Republicans both pander to non-whites and scrupulously avoid explicit appeals to white interests.

Republicans believe that if they don't pander to minorities, they will lose more *white* votes than they would gain. Republicans, moreover, believe that if they explicitly appeal to white interests, they will also lose more white votes than they will gain. It's all about the white vote in the end.

Republicans probably also think that a visible Whexit of race-conscious whites would *help* their reputation and boost their support among white normies. Indeed, there was probably rejoicing at Trump campaign headquarters when Richard Spencer endorsed Joe Biden. Republicans don't want the support of racist whites. They probably think that the Alt Right cost Trump more votes than it gained him, both by turning off Republicans and energizing the Left. You know damn well that's what Republican campaign strategists told Trump. They might have even told the truth.

For the sake of argument, however, let's consider the possibility that a Whexit might actually hurt the Republicans. If we really can hurt them, won't that change their calculations? People, after all, learn from suffering. That's why we spank naughty children.

But human psychology is more complicated than that, particularly when morality gets involved. If people merely acted out of rational self-interest, then a race-conscious Whexit might indeed change Republican calculations in future elections.

But this argument leaves out the whole reason we are in this situation in the first place: the moral consensus that appealing to white ethnic interests, and only white ethnic interests, is simply *evil*. Normie Republicans regard us as evil. *They would rather lose without us than win with us.* Simply hurting them will not change their minds, because *people will put up with quite a lot of suffering if they think it is moral.*

Obviously, the only way to change Republican behavior is to attack the anti-racist moral consensus that lies behind it. But changing the moral consensus of society is a metapolitical task, not a political one. Until anti-white racism loses moral power, racially-conscious whites will not gain political power.

Talk of a race-conscious Whexit seems to be premised on the claim that "the Alt Right memed Trump into the White House." If we managed to elect Trump, they reason, then we can also defeat him.

This argument is a tissue of delusion and puffery. The proper response came from Elle "Innsmouth" Reeve when she told Richard Spencer, "I think you're a fraud." The claim we put Trump in the White House is not based on any factual analysis of the electorate or the actual election results. We don't know how many White Nationalists are out there, where they are located, or how politically active they are. We are an unknown quantity, so the Republicans can hardly factor us into their calculations.

But they can very plausibly claim that we were a net detriment to Trump because we turned off some Republicans and energized Democrats to vote against him. They may even have data to support it. Until we do actual studies of the electorate, we cannot refute them or make any plausible claims about our electoral clout. And, even if we could, the Republicans would still prefer to lose without us rather than win with us.

The only thing that will change that is a *moral* revolution. Until then, all white political organizing will be impeded by a gale-force moral headwind—and wignat talk of Whexit is just spitting into it.

Race-conscious whites are not going to change Republican voting patterns by staying at home and pretending they are "exercising power." Again, we are not going to gain political power without overthrowing the moral consensus that white racism, and only white racism, is the wickedest thing in the world. That's a metapolitical task. It requires changing people's minds. It is an educational project, which requires that we stay online and able to reach the public.

This is why online freedom is under attack from Leftist-controlled corporations. But we still have the First Amendment. Trump should have done something about tech censorship years ago. He has made some efforts to protect online freedom, but too little too late. It could cost him the election. If Biden is elected, however, we can expect erosion of the First Amendment and no relief on tech censorship. This is one of the main reasons why it is crucially important for White Nationalists to re-elect Trump.

The other crucial reason is that Trump has slowed white demographic decline, which buys us time. We need to convert anti-whites to pro-whites. If we can get enough people on our side, we can save our race in America. Trump gives us more time to do that, while Biden will speed up the Great Replacement by opening the borders and putting tens of millions of illegals on the path to citizenship and voting. The goal of the Left is to make any form of white populist resistance electorally impossible. Racially aware whites would have to be stupid, crazy, or evil to support that.

Don't be a chump. Vote Trump.

Counter-Currents, November 3, 2020

Trump, Without Illusions or Apologies

I know many decent, race-conscious whites who want to sit out the upcoming election. I want to change their minds. I want all of my American readers who can vote to vote for Donald Trump. I understand why people are upset with Trump. He had a great opportunity to really turn things around, and he bungled it. Beyond that, his campaign has been terrible. His pandering to non-whites while taking white votes for granted is especially disgusting. He really deserves to lose.

But Trump *did* keep a lot of his promises. He did many good things for whites and avoided many bad things for whites. For a rundown, see Jared Taylor's analysis "Biden or Trump? How Should We Prepare?"[1] (I also endorse the analyses by Kevin MacDonald[2] and Spencer Quinn.[3]) It seems like a failure measured by the standard of what we would have liked Trump to have done, what *needed* to be done to save America. But it is still an improvement, especially when measured by what would likely have happened under a Hillary Clinton administration.

A Biden-Harris administration would undo everything good Trump has done and work to accelerate white demographic decline, i.e., the Great Replacement or white genocide. Their goal is a permanent Leftist one-party state ruling over a non-white majority, at which point it will be

---

[1] Jared Taylor, "Biden or Trump? How Should We Prepare?" *American Renaissance*," October 23, 2020

[2] Kevin MacDonald, "Why It's Important for Trump to Win," *The Occidental Observer*, October 21, 2020.

[3] Spencer J. Quinn, "My Case for Trump," *Counter-Currents*, October 22, 2020.

impossible for whites to preserve ourselves within the present political system. Biden has already promised an amnesty and path to citizenship for eleven million illegal aliens. Of course the real number is probably twenty or thirty million. Biden deserves to lose even more than Trump does.

A Biden-Harris administration would accelerate the already alarming trends toward totalitarianism. There will be more private censorship and deplatforming. There will be more state incursions on our First and Second Amendment rights. It will be increasingly difficult for white advocates to say or do anything to turn these trends around.

If Biden wins, you will have an "Oh my God, what have I done?" moment that you will have to live down for the rest of your life. Having elected militant and "competent" anti-whites, perhaps you will repent while sharing a cell with Richard Spencer in Guantanamo.

The bottom line: If Trump loses, we all lose. If Trump wins, we have more of a chance to win. Ultimately, white identitarians are the only ones who can save white America. Trump was just an opportunity, just a warmup act. When he is gone, real national populists will be waiting to take the stage. But that future may be canceled if Biden wins. So vote Trump.

Some people in reliably red or blue states might argue that their votes won't count anyway. I used to think that, but I was wrong. Although the election is determined by electoral college votes, remember when Hillary beat Trump in the popular vote? Suddenly, the entire establishment developed constitutional amnesia and treated it as a great affront to democracy that millions of illegals voting in California could not put Hillary in the White House. Trump needs every vote he can get, popular and electoral. So get out there and deliver them.

Some people argue that the Republicans will never stop

ignoring whites and pandering to non-whites unless white people stop voting for them. The sad truth is that they will still do the same thing even if people *do* stop voting for them, *because they would rather lose than be racist*. We can't change these people's minds by rolling up a newspaper and swatting them like bad dogs. We'll only change their minds by destroying the fake moral code that says that racism is the worst thing in the world, but only for whites. That's one of our main tasks at *Counter-Currents*. Voting for Trump will make it easier for us to stay on the web and fight this crucial intellectual battle.

The cargo cults of Melanesia started during the Second World War when the Allies dropped supplies from airplanes. To this day, the natives hope to make the white man rain down free stuff upon them again by building thatched models of airplanes. Some white advocates seem to think that engaging in a cargo-cult imitation of petulant blacks will make the GOP rain down favors on us.

But it won't happen. The GOP knows that white people are the adults in the room. We think about the common good. We think about the long run. We think about the lesser of two evils. And we pull the GOP lever once again. That's what I want you to do this time. Vote for the Orange Man. It's important.

There are people on the Right criticizing Trump for being pro-Jewish. As if there had ever been any reason to expect otherwise. I didn't vote for Trump because I thought he would be anti-Jewish. I voted for him because he was significantly more pro-white than his opponent. That is still the case.

There are people on the Right criticizing Trump for being pro-black, pro-Hispanic, and pro-Asian. As if there had ever been any reason to expect otherwise. I didn't vote for Trump because I thought he would be anti-black, etc. I voted for him because he was significantly more pro-white than his opponent. That is still the case.

There are people on the Right who condemn Trump for being pro-gay. Imagine thinking that Trump would make the Republicans less gay. But, again, I didn't vote for Trump because I thought he would be anti-gay. I voted for him because he was significantly more pro-white than his opponent. That is still the case.

Some of the same people who hold Trump to these delusional standards mock the delusions of the MAGAtards, Qtards, and other Trump cultists.

But I have no illusions about Donald Trump. I have no apologetics to offer for his failings. Grading him by absolute standards, he deserves to lose. But elections are graded on a curve. And Biden deserves to lose more. So I want you to do the reasonable thing, the responsible thing, the right thing, the *white* thing, and cast your vote for Donald Trump.

What do I think is going to happen?

This election was the Democrats' to lose, simply based on demographics. But with the Biden-Harris ticket, they might have been stupid enough to lose it. It was a miracle that Trump was elected in the first place. It will be an even bigger miracle if he gets reelected. But my gut is telling me that he will pull it off.

The only thing I am certain of, however, is that no matter who wins, the other half of the electorate will declare the result illegitimate: Democrats, because they are entitled brats. Republicans, with very good reason. If Biden wins, it will be because of demographic replacement, ballot fraud, and tech censorship. If Biden wins, he cheated, and Trump should not concede under any circumstances.

What are we going to do at *Counter-Currents* if Biden is elected? More of the same. The headwinds will be stronger, so we will just have to work harder—all of us will, including you, dear reader. But if Biden does win, tens of millions of white Americans are going to wake up to the fact that their country has been stolen—and their future as a people mortally threatened—by demographic displacement and an opposition handicapped by the delusion that racism is the greatest evil, but only when it favors white people. There will be a lot more people receptive to our arguments. But it will be much more difficult to reach them. Perhaps it will be too late.

Counter-Currents, October 30, 2020

IS AMERICA A BANANA REPUBLIC NOW?

This year's US Presidential contest is between the Republican Party and the Banana Republican Party, formerly known as the Democrats. As I write this, the Democrats are trying to destroy American democracy because the people have disappointed them once again. Donald Trump is the rightful victor of this election, and if Biden ends up with more votes, it is only because he cheated. Trump should not concede under any circumstances until all challenges have been exhausted.

Let's review how the Democrats are trying to destroy American democracy.

First, the only way to ensure both the integrity of the electoral rolls and the secrecy of people's votes is for registered voters to show up in person (to prove they are alive) with valid identification papers (to prove that they are who they say they are), then receive a ballot. So that their choices remain secret, all ballots must be identical. There can be no numbers that would allow a given ballot to be connected with a given voter.

Democrats violate this process flagrantly in two ways.

First, they object to voter identification, which they say is "racist," because many black and brown people somehow can't manage to get proper identification—yet the opinions of these people are supposed to matter just as much as the opinions of those who are intelligent and responsible enough to secure proper identification.

Second, Democrats are champions of ballots that are simply mailed out to voters then mailed back in. When I lived in Washington State, I received the ballots of the four previous residents of my apartment. In the lobby of my building was a trash can, filled with discarded ballots sent to previous occupants. In the post office around the corner, trash cans were overflowing with discarded ballots. There is nothing to prevent these ballots from being collected and filled out by anyone. We are told that this is impossible because the signatures on the envelopes must match the signatures of the voters on record, a system that can be defeated by dishonest or lazy poll workers. The only way ensure that mail-in ballots are filled out by the actual voter is to make every ballot trackable, which violates the whole idea of secret balloting.

It is an idiotic system, designed by corrupt Democratic machines to destroy democracy. COVID-19 was the Democrats' excuse to push to expand mail-in balloting this year, corrupting the electoral process even more.

Sadly, Republicans have been too weak and too stupid to challenge these obvious frauds.

The integrity of the election has also been compromised by the press and tech giants (Twitter, Facebook, Google), who are throttling the free flow of information and the free expression of opinions because they are open partisans of the Left. Democracy is obviously compromised when people can't make informed decisions.

The integrity of this election has also been compromised by months of Left-wing violence, followed by threats of intensified violence if Trump is re-elected, including from Joe Biden himself. People can't make free and informed decisions if they are threatened with violence. Republicans disproportionately vote in person on election day. Yet across the country, in Democratic-run cities that have been convulsed by months of violence, these voters had to ask themselves if they could safely go to the polls.

The deepest form of Democratic voter fraud is the Great Replacement: the demographic swamping of white America with non-whites, who vote for Democrats more than seven out of ten times. Every non-white immigrant dilutes the political power of white Americans. Every non-white immigrant lowers the wages of white Americans. That's why they are here.

When we point this out, the Left dismisses it as a "conspiracy theory." But they also openly gloat about how well it is working.

Democracy is based on the sovereignty of the people. *These are not the American people.* They are scabs stealing our wages and ringers stealing our votes. Democracy is about making elites accountable to the people. Non-white immigration is a plot by the elites to replace uppity whites with brown helots who will be grateful to the employers and bureaucrats who dispense their diminished wages and benefits.

In a democracy, the people elect the elites to serve the people's interests. Democracy no longer exists when the elites decide to choose a new people to serve elite interests. Non-white immigration delegitimizes democracy. Time to end this farce.

What should Trump do?

If I were Trump, I would sit down with Biden, lay out every detail of the corruption charges that can and will be lodged against him and his family. Then I would offer him a deal: concede. High-mindedly refuse to be made president by an undemocratic process. In exchange, all charges will go away, and Joe can nap the rest of his life away. It would be worth it to save the country from bloodshed.

Trump certainly has nothing to lose. If he concedes, the vindictive Democrats will try to destroy him and his family. Machiavelli recommends always leaving one's enemy a way to retreat, since if his back is against the wall, he will fight even harder, and even if you win, your victory will be far more expensive. Trump's back is to the wall. He has no choice but to fight, but he should leave Biden a way to retreat.

Even if Biden took such a deal, Trump should not start

his second term under a cloud of doubt about the real will of the electorate. Thus we should pinpoint every rotten precinct where fraud is taking place. Then we should throw out the results and rerun the election, under fully transparent conditions, with international observers. The eligibility and identity of every voter needs to be verified.

If Democrats refuse, then America is officially a banana republic. Careful what you wish for, though. If the Democrats wish to discard the Constitution, then Trump and his supporters don't have to follow the rules either. In fact, quite a lot of them are looking for any excuse to take up arms. Banana republics are the original home of Right-wing death squads. They usually end up being ruled by strongmen. And in this race, Donald Trump is the strong man. Trump has been tweeting like a Latin dictator for years. He's ready to step into the role.

So I've got to ask the Democrats: Are you sure you want a banana republic?

Counter-Currents, November 4, 2020

AFTER THE ELECTION

Like many of you, I got caught up in the 2020 US presidential race. From Tuesday to Friday of election week, I was glued to the internet, biting my nails and hitting refresh like a rat in a Skinner box.

I knew the establishment would try to call the election for Biden as soon as it was plausible, and as soon as that happened, I managed to wrench myself away from the coverage to collect my thoughts.

I understand why many race-conscious whites are depressed by the outcome thus far. A lot is riding on this election. It really does matter to us who wins, because Trump actually slowed white demographic decline while Biden promises to accelerate it dramatically as well as to attack our First and Second Amendment freedoms. It is disgusting to see massive voter fraud. It is also disgusting to watch the gloating of Leftists and the Right-wing idiots who enable them.

But their celebrations may be premature. Trump is still fighting, and he may still win.

Our lives may change a great deal depending on the outcome of this election. But at a certain point, one has to disengage. At this point, there is almost nothing I can do to affect the outcome one way or another. That is in the hands of President Trump, his lawyers, and countless officials, judges, and legislators all over the country. If the time comes for visible demonstrations of public support, I will take part. But in the meantime, I need to get back to work. We all do.

What is our work? At *Counter-Currents*, it is laying the intellectual groundwork for White Nationalism, meaning the right of all white peoples to their own sovereign homelands. This project requires establishing the philosophical and scientific case for ethnonationalism, the political necessity of ethnonationalism for whites, a vision of how white ethnonationalism will work, and a plausible account of how to get there from here. We also must constantly dismantle enemy arguments. Finally, we need to foster white consciousness, pride, and community.

Our work remains the same no matter who is the next President of the US. But the obstacles and opportunities we will encounter will change dramatically. There are basically four possible outcomes.

The worst-case scenario is that Biden steals the White House, and the Democrats take control of the Senate. The Left would then move to establish a one-party state: opening the borders, amnestying tens of millions of existing invaders and giving them votes, adding states to the union, changing the Senate rules, packing the Supreme Court, and weakening the First and Second Amendments. A lot depends on the Georgia Senatorial races in January.

The second worst scenario is that Biden steals the White House, but the Republicans hold on to the Senate. We would avoid a one-party state, but open borders and amnesty will still be likely. Tech censorship will go unabated. We will face state censorship and oppression. But the Second Amendment will probably be safe.

It is a real question whether Biden would have the stomach and political capital to push through anything radical with a divided congress and the stench of illegitimacy hanging over his regime. After all, he would be faced with four massive crises: the second wave of COVID, BLM and antifa riots, the economic depression caused by the first two, and a deep legitimacy crisis.

Trumpism has not been repudiated. In fact, it has gained support. Biden was not elected in a free and fair election. The country remains deeply divided and bitterly polarized. This is no atmosphere in which to push deeply divisive policies. Besides, Biden is not a Leftist. He is the Senator from the credit card industry: a cynical, corrupt, greedy neoliberal hack.

I hope this is true, but I wouldn't bank on it. There would be no one-party state in the second scenario, but both parties are equally committed to globalism and elitism. They are also equally opposed to nationalism and populism. Hence their hysteria over Trump. He was an existential threat to the entire political establishment. The establishment not only wants to stop Trump, they want to prevent anything like Trumpism from ever arising again. Thus I would predict a bipartisan consensus around open borders and amnesty, as well as the censorship and repression of nationalist and populist ideas and organizations.

The third worst scenario is that Trump holds onto the White House, but the Democrats take the Senate. At that point, Trump and Pence might face impeachment based on any number of crackpot conspiracies, and then we are back to some version scenario one.

The best-case scenario is that Trump holds onto the White House, and the Republicans hold on to the Senate. Trump was profoundly disappointing in his first term, and there is no reason to expect anything better in his second. But even if we only get more of the same, Trump gives us the time and the freedom to press forward with our work. Trump gives us time by slowing demographic decline. He gives us freedom by resisting erosion of our First and Second Amendment rights. It is foolish to hope for more.

Are there any downsides to having Trump in the White House?

When there is a Republican in the White House, it tends to make people of a conservative bent feel like things are alright. Thus they become politically disengaged and complacent. This was also true of people of a nationalist and populist bent during Trump's first term. This is bad for White Nationalists, however, because slowing demographic decline is not enough. We need to halt and reverse it. That requires that we heighten our people's sense of danger. One could argue that the complacency fostered by Trump in the White House would make it harder for us.

But let's be honest here. In this scenario, the fault is not Trump's. The fault is not his supporters'. The fault is our own. We simply need to work harder to persuade more people of the necessity of more radical solutions.

It is foolish to want Biden in the White House just to rile up seventy million Trump supporters. Yes, they would be much more receptive to our message. But we might be less capable of reaching them. They might also be too demoralized to act. The establishment, moreover, will be adding tens of millions of new facts on the ground. So we might convince more people there is a problem, but the problem might become too big to plausibly solve. I hope that doesn't happen. If it does, we will just work harder and adapt.

It is easy to get caught up in political contests, especially when important things are at stake. But we need to step back and remind ourselves that the most important issues in any political system are precisely what the parties *agree* upon. Before Trump, both parties agreed never to compete with each other on immigration and globalization. Trump's greatest accomplishment as a candidate was simply to reject that consensus.

In this election, Trump was hamstrung by a point where he *agrees* with the political establishment. Trump pandered frantically to blacks, Hispanics, Asians, and Jews. But he would not even "dog-whistle" to white interests and concerns. Instead, Trump denounced white identity politics, but not identity-politics for non-whites.

In short, Trump bought into the fake moral absolute that there's nothing worse than "racism," but only when white people practice it.

Substantial numbers of white Americans reject the idea that identity politics is bad only when white people engage in it. They have positive white identities, feel that whites are being discriminated against by the system, and think that it is necessary and moral for whites to take our own side in a fight. They are ready for white identity politics. But neither the Republicans nor the Democrats will represent them.

Why did the entire political establishment—Right and Left—fold in the face of months of Black Lives Matter and antifa rioting? For the same reason that the establishment is united in opposition to white identity politics: the dominance of a flagrant moral double standard that white identity politics is evil and non-white identity politics is good. Until that false moral imperative is dethroned, our path will be blocked while our enemies will be free to destroy every white nation.

The moral revolution has to come first.

Overturning false moral principles and upholding true ones is the work of moral philosophy. It's an absolutely necessary part of *metapolitics*, which is our job here at *Counter-Currents*. So let's all get back to work.

Counter-Currents, November 11, 2020

Goodbye, Mr. Trump

What should the white identitarian agenda be in the post-Trump era?

1. The Moral Case for White Identity Politics

Trump faced many enemies, including the Democrats, the Republicans, the "deep state," the far Left, Black Lives Matter, and the mainstream media. But the greatest impediment to Making America Great Again is the idea that identity politics is good for every group except white people, the people who made America great in the first place.

White identity politics is condemned as "racism," which is the worst thing in the world, but only if practiced by white people for their own benefit. Racism is fine if practiced by non-whites. It is even fine if practiced by whites for the benefit of non-whites.

This dogma is the barrier between white identity politics and the entire political mainstream. It bars white identitarians from polite society and political power. Trump himself was hamstrung by accepting this dogma, and it became increasingly dominant over the four years of his presidency. Trump's dumbest and most undignified decisions—criminal justice reform, the ludicrous Platinum Plan, championing criminal rappers like ASAP Rocky, Lil Wayne, and Kodak Black—were rather expensive premiums for insurance against the charge of "racism."

Tearing down this false moral imperative must be the top priority for white identitarians in the post-Trump era.

Large numbers of white Americans have positive racial identities, believe that whites are systematically discriminated against by the current system, and believe that whites should organize politically to secure our interests. But nobody in the political establishment will represent these people because of the dogma that identity politics is bad only when white people benefit from it. Once we destroy that dogma, the floodwaters of white identity politics will wash away our entire rotten establishment.

We must also criticize the dominant Right-wing critique and evasion of white identity politics, namely the "colorblind" civic nationalism that unites the mainstream Right from country-club Republicans to QAnon believers and militia groups.

For instance, why not just take the Tucker Carlson approach of pleading with non-whites to stop practicing identity politics and just be "Americans"? The simple answer is that they won't. When you are armed with a knife and your enemies are armed with guns, how likely are they to throw down their guns and fight "fair," even if you ask them really nicely?

The only answer to anti-white identity politics is pro-white identity politics. We must take a gun to a gunfight. Thus we need to argue that white identity politics is not just *moral* but also *necessary*, because if we don't adopt it, we will be destroyed. And because white identity politics is both *moral* and *necessary*, it is also *inevitable*.[1]

2. Race Realism

Our second most urgent priority is to promote the widespread acceptance of the reality of biological differences between the races. The opposite of race realism is the dogma that race is a "social construct."[2] People advocate social constructivism because if race differences are

---

[1] For a more thorough discussion, see Greg Johnson, "White Identity Politics: Inevitable, Necessary, Moral," *White Identity Politics*.

[2] See Greg Johnson, "Why Race Is Not a Social Construct," in *Toward a New Nationalism* and *It's Okay to Be White: The Best of Greg Johnson* (Hollywood: Ministry of Truth, 2020).

biological, they can only be altered biologically, whereas if they are socially constructed, they can be changed through social policy.

Why must we defend race realism? Because our enemies assume that the races are equal, thus when different races—most prominently blacks—fail spectacularly to flourish in America, the problem must be with the American people and social system, specifically with white people, who created America. The alleged cause of black failure is white "racism." Racism means institutional discrimination as well as the prejudice and ill will of individuals.

Because blacks continue to fail even after anti-black discrimination has been replaced by pro-black discrimination, more "occult" forms of racism have been hypothesized, such as "systemic racism," the eradication of which requires ever more radical forms of social engineering.[3]

Whites, however, seem to be quite incompetent at erecting systems of "white supremacy" and "white privilege," given that visible non-white groups like East and South Asians now outperform whites in terms of education, income, and law-abidingness—the very areas in which blacks lag far behind.

The best explanation for why some non-whites flourish and others fail under our "system of white supremacy" is the existence of biological race differences. Differences in intelligence and sociopathic personality traits between the races, which are largely biological, predict virtually all differences in performance, regardless of systemic discrimination and personal prejudices.

The assault on "white racism," "white privilege," and "white supremacism" will only intensify in the post-Trump era, so we must intensify our efforts to counter it. Race realism is a stake through the heart of this poisonous ide-

---

[3] See Greg Johnson, "The Very Idea of White Privilege," in *White Identity Politics* and *It's Okay to Be White*.

ology, and we must drive it home.

3. Anti-Violence

The Biden regime was installed after a stolen election in a Potemkin inaugural guarded by tens of thousands of troops who were vetted for political loyalty. That's because the American establishment is terrified of the American people. The Biden regime and its hysterical cheerleaders in Congress and the media want to treat seventy-plus million white Trump supporters as potential domestic terrorists.

This is a terrible mistake. It is false, it is unjust, and it will further alienate and radicalize the half of the electorate that owns probably 85% of the firearms in the country.

There will be blood. There will probably be more senseless shooting sprees targeting innocent civilians at places of worship. But now that the establishment is cracking down on antifa as well, politicians, journalists, and tech oligarchs may well start dying too.

Whatever happens, white identitarians need to stay out of it.

The enemy controls all the leading institutions of our society. They control all the instruments of coercion, including the military, the police, even the dog catchers. They can literally create all the money they need out of thin air. The only thing they lack is truth and justice. Their policies are premised on falsehoods and moral outrages and lead to disastrous consequences, which they then lie about, cover up, and blame on others, often the victims.

By contrast, we control only a few beleaguered outposts on the internet. We have no armies. We have almost no money. Our only advantages over our enemies are truth, justice, and the credibility that comes from standing up for them. We are the only ones offering a workable alternative to the catastrophic consequences of multiculturalism and globalization.

Given such a correlation of forces, only a fool would choose to take up arms, since we can't win that way. And only a damned fool would throw away our moral advantage by targeting innocents.

Since our movement's primary way of changing the world is through speaking the truth fearlessly, preserving our freedom of speech is absolutely paramount. Right-wing violence leads to the erosion of freedom of speech in two ways. First, it causes moral panics that lead to deplatforming by private companies. Second, it provides pretexts for further state erosion of the First Amendment's protection of free speech.

Right-wing violence does not weaken the system. It strengthens it. This is why the system goes out of its way to manufacture Right-wing violence, which is why we should treat everyone who talks about violence as an enemy *agent provocateur*.

The Biden regime will intensify the causes of Right-wing violence: diversity, white dispossession, censorship, repression, and outright entrapment. Thus we must intensify our attempts to warn our people away from violence.

4. Remember the Four Ds

In the book *National Populism: The Revolt Against Liberal Democracy*, Roger Eatwell and Matthew Goodwin argue that the rise of national populist figures like Donald Trump are caused by long-term social trends that they call the "four Ds": *distrust* of the establishment by the people, *destruction* of white societies by multiculturalism and immigration, *deprivation* caused by economic globalization, and *dealignment* of voters from the center-Left and center-Right parties that dominated the post-war era.[4]

---

[4] See Greg Johnson, "National Populism Is Here to Stay,"

We can contribute to the national populist ferment by raising *awareness* of the destruction and deprivation caused by multiculturalism and globalization, thereby promoting distrust of the establishment and dealignment with its political parties.

5. Building Alternative Platforms

The first four items in this list have something in common: They are ideas that everyone reading this can help spread to one extent or another. Another important priority requires specialized talents that only few people have: building alternative platforms.

Trump had four years to tackle big tech censorship, deplatforming, and election meddling with legislation, regulation, and the presidential bully pulpit. For two of those years, he had a Republican congress. He never took the problem seriously until it was too late. This is Trump's greatest failure. All we need is free speech. We'll take care of the rest. I have no doubt that we can win every fair public debate. That's why our enemies want to shut us down.

Biden owes his presidency in part to big tech's abuses of power. Thus there is no hope of a legislative solution under his watch. This means that dissidents are on our own. We really are going to have to build our own YouTube, build our own Twitter, build our own Facebook, build our own banks, etc. The fate of Parler shows how difficult it will be. But it is good practice for building our own country in the end.

There are, of course, many other things that people can do to genuinely advance our cause.

For instance, it would be useful to have a think tank to study social trends and craft nationalist policies. It would also be useful to have our own public interest law firm to protect our rights and attack our enemies through lawfare. But we don't yet have the money and the personnel for such institutions.

6. Connecting with Our Constituency

Once we clarify our message and priorities, we then have to find our audience and connect with them in order to convert them to our way of thinking.

Our movement is small, poor, and constantly harried by our enemies. Thus we have to make our efforts count. What segment of the electorate is most likely to be receptive to white identity politics: Trump voters or Biden voters? Obviously, Trump voters. They are our natural constituency. How, then, can we connect with Trump voters in order to lead them toward the truth?

First, it helps if one supported Trump's candidacy rather than sitting on the sidelines or voting to hand the country to Joe Biden, so he can treat Trump supporters as domestic terrorists and kick the Great Replacement into overdrive.

Second, it helps to give Trump just credit for his virtues and accomplishments. We can't lose sight of the fact that Trump is fervently admired by tens of millions, and with some justification. Beyond that, the people who fervently hate Trump don't hate him for his flaws and failings. They hate him for his virtues. They hate him because in their minds he stands for whiteness. In short, they hate him because they hate us. If you sound like these people, very few Trump voters will take you seriously, even if you have legitimate grievances.

Trump has a long enough list of flaws and failings. One does not need to embroider it. Thus it is very foolish to dip a broad brush in pure bile and pen embittered diatribes that make Rachel Maddow seem sober by comparison. The lying press has been doing this for five years now, and it has not destroyed Trump's credibility. It has simply destroyed its own credibility. There's a lesson in that.

Pouring unjust scorn on Trump looks like an attempt to cozy up with the enemies of the people. How do you expect the people to take you seriously?

Third, stop repeating establishment lies about the election. As much as I would like to say that Trump lost because he ran a conventional Republican campaign—pandering to every interest group except whites—it simply isn't true. Trump won the last election.

It upsets me that Trump campaigned and won as a Republican not a populist, because that will simply encourage Republicans to continue ignoring the predictable consequences of white demographic decline, namely, the doom of their party. But it does prove my contention that Trump could have won in 2016 on a conventional Republican platform, because that's exactly how he won in 2020.

Trump voters have just seen their votes negated by massive and systematic fraud. The founders, of course, put provisions in place to prevent fraudulent votes from counting. For these safeguards to work, Trump only needed hundreds of Republicans on the state and federal level to have the courage and integrity to follow the law. In short, he didn't have a chance.

Trump was denied his rightful place in the White House by Democratic fraud and Republican collusion. The lion was brought down by a swarm of jackals, hyenas, and rats. It has never been clearer that the two-party system is a sham. There is a single political establishment that makes an art of never giving the people what they want. This is a wonderful lesson for populists to drive home. But we can't teach it by repeating establishment lies, namely that the election was honest and the attempts to stop the steal were a fraud.

When it became clear that the fix was in on January 6th, a few dozen of the thousands of pro-Trump marchers broke onto the Capitol building, causing a panicked evacuation of the congress. Other protestors were apparently ushered in by the police. Most of the people who entered the building were Trump supporters. But there was at least one antifa agitator as well. Some came to protest. Some came to commit crimes. Some got caught up in the moment. Some surely thought they were being invited on a free tour of the Capitol. One young woman, Ashli Babbitt, a QAnon supporter, was shot and killed by a police officer, even though she obviously posed no threat. Many of the protestors merely sauntered around the Capitol taking selfies, then dispersed on their own.

The events at the Capitol have been called a "riot," a "siege," and an "insurrection." In most cases, it was simply unauthorized tourism, and in some cases it seemed fully authorized. In truth, it was a "mostly peaceful protest," but the lying press has turned that phrase into a euphemism for genuine riots and insurrections. We don't need to endorse illegal activities or bad optics to say that we understand these people's frustration.

Beyond that, the establishment's reaction is absurdly exaggerated. A few of the marchers committed serious crimes, so punish them. But the rest deserve the utmost leniency because patriotic protest and civil disobedience are parts of every healthy democracy. Leniency, however, is reserved only for Left-wing protesters who break into the Capitol, as well as black and antifa mobs. The Capitol protestors are being railroaded by a hysterical establishment, in which Democrats and Republicans again have closed ranks. It is a wonderful lesson for newly receptive normies. But they aren't going to listen to people who are cheerleading the betrayal and martyrdom of the protestors.

Trump has also been impeached a second time on the bogus charge of inciting the "insurrection" by Democrats and Republicans voting together. If he is convicted and barred from seeking office again, it will only happen because of Republican collusion as well.

Convicting Trump and barring him from seeking office would be a gross injustice. It would also be a serious political blunder from which we can profit. First, it would further underscore the fact that we are governed by a political cartel. Second, it would permanently sour many Trump supporters on the Republican Party, which needs to be thoroughly purged by populists or simply replaced by something new. Third, it would clear the way for more articulate, cunning, and decisive populist leaders to emerge.

Goodbye, Mr. Trump. I hate to see it end this way. But you will be vindicated. You will be avenged. You started something. You gave voice to the millions of Americans victimized by globalization, open borders, and military adventurism. You got the Left to drop the mask of sanity and civility. You exposed the dishonesty of the press. You showed us that the Republicans are a false opposition. You forced the deep state to slither out of the shadows. You showed the world that the people do not rule America.

Instead, we are ruled by a corrupt and decadent elite that hates us—and that hates you because you represented us. The people don't rule if our votes don't count, the vote counters rule. The people don't rule if our voices are stifled, the censors rule. The laws do not rule if they can be applied selectively, the judges rule. But we're awake now. We are not going to forget.

You unleashed populist forces that will not be satisfied until the globalists are swept from power and government of the people, by the people, for the people is restored. There's no guarantee we will win. But if we win, historians looking back at the restoration of popular government in America will say that it began with Donald Trump.

Counter-Currents, January 27, 2021

ANARCHO-TYRANNY IN OSLO

The Scandza Forum is a nationalist metapolitical organization that has put on conferences in Sweden, Norway, and Denmark. It was founded in 2017 and is led by Fróði Midjord.

Until recently, I had spoken at every Scandza Forum event. But on Saturday, October 12, 2019, I was prevented from speaking at the Scandza Forum's second conference in Copenhagen by a raging mob of communists (complete with the Soviet flag).

Then, on Saturday, November 2, I was prevented from speaking at the second Scandza conference in Norway by the Norwegian government itself, although it is clear that the state had been gaslighted into action by a false report written by antifa and acted upon by collaborators in the government.

Scandza's inaugural event in Oslo, on July 1, 2017, was the first of its type in Norway, and our Norwegian friends were anxious for us to come back. The theme of the new conference was "Human Biodiversity," i.e., the variations in genetic potential between the sexes and races. Human biodiversity undermines the bedrock assumption of modern egalitarianism, namely that differences in social outcomes between the races and sexes can be explained by mutable human ideas and institutions, so that by changing ideas and institutions, we can arrive at an egalitarian society. If, however, different social outcomes are based on biological differences, then they will persist even after all forms of unequal treatment are removed. Past that point, egalitarian social engineering projects are based on delusions and can only multiply the miseries of the world.

The speakers included Dr. Kevin MacDonald, Professor Emeritus of Psychology at California State University, Long Beach, talking about his new book *Individualism and the Western Liberal Tradition*; Dr. Helmuth Nyborg, Professor Emeritus of Psychology at the University of Aarhus and a prolific author of scientific books and articles; and Dr. Edward Dutton, editor of *Mankind Quarterly* and author of many books and articles.

My talk was entitled "The Very Idea of White Privilege."[1] I argue that the science of human biodiversity undermines the idea of white privilege as used by the Left, but I also argue that there is a sense of white privilege that is grounded in human biodiversity—namely, that whites naturally create societies that are more comfortable for whites than other races—but that this is inevitable, and there is nothing morally objectionable about it.

When I arrived in Oslo on Thursday, October 31st, I learned that *Filter Nyheter*, a communist ("antifa") blog, had published an article about me entitled "Hailed Breivik's Rationale for the July 22 Terror—Now he is Going to Oslo to Speak for 'White Nationalists'" ("Hyllet Breiviks begrunnelse for 22. juli-terroren—nå skal han til Oslo for å tale for «hvite nasjonalister»"),[2] in which the authors Harald S. Kungtveit and Jonas Skybakmoen write:

> Johnson has previously expressed support for how Anders Behring Breivik justified the July 22 attacks in 2011 in his trial, referred to the terror as "necessary," and has described at length the killing of Labor Party politicians as a legitimate means to fight "non-white immigration."

---

[1] Greg Johnson, "The Very Idea of White Privilege," *White Identity Politics* and *It's Okay to Be White*.

[2] Harald S. Kungtveit and Jonas Skybakmoen, "Hyllet Breiviks begrunnelse for 22. juli-terroren – nå skal han til Oslo for å tale for «hvite nasjonalister»," *Filter Nyheter*, October 31, 2019.

This is a complete inversion of the truth, as any honest person reading my statements on Breivik can see for himself.[3] I did not "support" Breivik's justification for terrorism. I carefully analyzed and criticized it. In referring to Breivik's crimes as "necessary," I am referring to Breivik's views, not my own. The whole point of my article is to argue that killing Labor Party politicians—or any form of terrorism, for that matter—is *not* a legitimate means to fight non-white immigration.

The authors additionally claim, "In the text, Johnson appears to be fine with much of Breivik's reasoning," which is laughable, given that my conclusion is that Breivik's arguments do *not* establish a case for terrorism, and I also offer my own powerful arguments *against* terrorism.

Furthermore, the authors claim that "Johnson criticizes Breivik's manifesto—not for the calls for more right-wing terrorist actions—but because the text was too long and unmanageable." Actually, I criticize his manifesto for *both* reasons.

When the authors assert that I "respect" Breivik, they leave out some key contextual details. My first essay on Breivik is utterly scathing. When Breivik went on trial, however, I admitted to gaining "a strange new respect" for him, because I thought he conducted himself in a dignified manner and offered a more coherent rationale for his actions than in his manifesto. But first of all, this respect was *relative to my initial very negative impression of Breivik*. I had, in effect, raised him a few rungs in hell. Furthermore, as is clear to anyone who reads my article, thinking slightly better of Beivik did not alter my conclu-

---

[3] Greg Johnson, "Anders Behring Breivik: The Neoconservative Rambo" and "Breivik: A Strange New Respect," *Confessions of a Reluctant Hater*, 2nd expanded ed. (San Francisco: Counter-Currents, 2016).

sion that he failed to make a case for terrorism. Nor did it alter my own reasons for thinking terrorism is a terrible idea. Thus to flatly say that I "respect" Breivik is fundamentally deceptive. It is simply a lie.

I was left wondering. Were Kungtveit and Skybakmoen dishonest or just very, very stupid? Dishonesty seems the most charitable and likely explanation.

Later the same day, the same authors published another blog post, "Terrorist Researcher thinks Norway Should Deny Breivik Admirers Entry before Conference in Oslo" ("Terrorforsker mener Norge bør nekte Breivik-beundrer innreise før konferanse i Oslo").[4] Apparently the authors had shown their first lying article to an "expert" who did not bother to check the veracity of their claims, perhaps from incompetence, perhaps from complicity:

> Now, the terrorist expert and senior researcher at the Defense Research Institute (FFI), Thomas Hegghammer, believes that Norway should consider the possibility of denying Johnson entry before the scheduled conference on Saturday—partly based on the statements above.
>
> "Of course, we should not overuse these types of decisions or act as opinion police. But at the same time, I think there must be a limit somewhere. One indicator in this case is that the only neo-Nazi organization in Norway, the 'Nordic Resistance Movement,' is advertising the event—and that one of the speakers has given explicit support to Breivik. There is something very unmusical about bringing in an American Anders Behring Breivik sympathizer to Oslo, just where the terrorist attack happened on

---

[4] Harald S. Kungtveit and Jonas Skybakmoen, "Terrorforsker mener Norge bør nekte Breivik-beundrer innreise før konferanse i Oslo," *Filter Nyheter*, October 31, 2019.

July 22," says Hegghammer to *Filter News*.

First of all, as we have seen, I am not an "Anders Behring Breivik sympathizer" "who has given explicit support of Breivik."

Second, it is entirely irrelevant that the Nordic Resistance Movement posted information about the event—if it actually did so. Nobody can control who links to or talks about one's events. Moreover, if a group links one's event, that does not imply that they endorse or agree with it, in whole or in part. And *a fortiori* it certainly does not imply that Scandza Forum—or the people speaking at it—endorse everyone who links to the event.

Of course, the quickest way to get Leftists to drop this silly idea that "Speaker X should be banned because the conference he is speaking at was promoted by a dissident site" is simply to post links to the next public appearances of Thomas Hegghammer, Harald S. Kungtveit, and Jonas Skybakmoen at *Counter-Currents*.

Naturally, I was a bit worried about this, for when Marxists lie, people die—many millions of people, actually.

So Fróði Midjord and I drafted a response to be translated into Norwegian and sent to the press.[5] I did not want

---

[5] The response, "Greg Johnson Arrested in Norway for Thoughtcrime," *Counter-Currents*, November 2, 2019, was published after I had been arrested. The version that appeared was not, therefore, given a final edit by my hand. If I had given it a final once-over, the sentence "I have always consistently condemned violence and terrorism" would have simply read "I have always consistently condemned terrorism." I have now corrected that sentence. Only pacifists "always" condemn violence. I think violence can sometimes be morally legitimate, for instance in cases of self-defense. But I have always condemned *terrorism* as a tool for white self-defense, for reasons outlined in many articles, which are listed in my response cited above.

the response published immediately, however, because I hoped the blog post would not reach the mainstream press. Responding might draw more attention to it. I hoped that this would-be smear campaign would die in the weeds on an obscure communist blog.

Friday came and went without much discussion of the *Filter Nyheter* posts. I spent the day working on *Counter-Currents*, putting the finishing touches on my talk for the next day, and then having dinner with the conference speakers and old friends.

On Saturday, I went on my own to the conference site, arriving at 10 a.m., well before the start. I was prevented from entering the Copenhagen Scandza Forum because when I showed up 30 minutes before the event was to start, the facility was already surrounded by a mob of communists. I got to talk to some old friends and meet some new people. Then Fróði came over and told me that the police were coming to arrest me.

Welcome to Norway!

I grabbed my coat to go out to meet them because I did not want them barging into the conference venue. Sure enough, there were two policemen at the door. I asked if I was going to be arrested. They said yes. I asked them what for, and they told me they could not tell me. Not knowing Norwegian law, I could not tell if this was irregular or not. It certainly *seemed* that way to me.

But these were not guys to be trifled with. I decided to comply so as not to cause a scene at the venue. The authorities always make it easier to comply with them (right up to the point when they shoot you in the back of the head). When I got in the car, I took out my phone to send a message to my friends. I was told I could not have a phone, so I handed it over. At that point, with one brief exception, the only people I talked to for the next 48 hours were police and my lawyer's assistant.

After several hours alone in a cell—without shoes, belt,

or eyeglasses—I spoke to two plainclothes policemen who produced a document in Norwegian. They then called a woman who is a professional interpreter who rendered the text into English over a speakerphone. I was told that I had been detained and would be expelled under a provision of the Immigration Act, section 126, first paragraph, second sentence, "for the sake of basic national interests or foreign policy considerations . . ." because it was deemed that "the ideological message" I was to convey at The Scandza Forum could "inspire the practice of politically motivated violence." Obviously, the *Filter Nyheter* blog posts had found sympathetic ears somewhere in the Norwegian security service.

The whole thing struck me as idiotic.

First, the Norwegian authorities somehow divined that my talk could inspire political violence *without knowing the contents or even the title of my talk*—which was, again, "The Very Idea of White Privilege."

Second, if the authorities had bothered to check the titles of my other Scandza Forum talks, they would have learned that the last talk I gave was entitled "Against Right-Wing Terrorism" (Stockholm, March 30, 2019).[6] Indeed, I am the author of a long list of articles criticizing terrorism by White Nationalists. If I am the silver-tongued persuader the Norwegian state thinks I am, then I should be credited with *reducing* the amount of terrorism in the world. (The talk I gave at the first Scandza Forum in Oslo was a critique of irony as an ethos.[7] Perhaps I will be blamed for an uptick in sincerity among Norwegian youth.)

Third, I was being detained and deported *not for some-*

---

[6] A revision of this talk, "Against White Nationalist Terrorism," is published in this volume, below.

[7] Greg Johnson, "Identity vs. Irony," *Counter-Currents*, August 23, 2017.

thing I said or did, but for *something that somebody else might do after hearing a speech that I had not yet given*. And remember that my speech was on white privilege, a topic that I feared was more likely to produce boredom than violence.

Fourth, one of Breivik's arguments for resorting to terrorism was the Norwegian establishment's suppression of freedom of speech about immigration and multiculturalism. My talk could not in any way be construed as a call for political violence. *But suppressing my freedom of speech is precisely the kind of policy that encourages desperate people to commit acts of terrorism*. As John F. Kennedy said, "Those who make peaceful revolution impossible will make violent revolution inevitable." Breivik repeated this idea, almost word for word, during his trial. Will these people ever learn?

A related thought also occurred to me. Kungtveit and Skybakmoen were clearly trying to smear me by linking me to Breivik. But what if linking us has the opposite effect? What if it does not decrease my credibility but instead increases Breivik's? After all, I am an intelligent, educated, articulate guy. I have written eleven books and hundreds of articles. I have published sixty books. I run a highly successful webzine. I have cultivated a large circle of writers and donors. Putting the lie out there that I endorsed Breivik might actually make some people take him more seriously. This increases the chance that copy-cats might commit terrorist acts.

In short, *the only possible way that my writings on Breivik could lead to terrorism is because of Kungtveit and Skybakmoen's lies*. I wonder if such a possibility ever occurred to them. If it did, would they have even cared? After all, *the advocates of repression feed off Right-wing terrorism*. It empowers them to oppress us, so why wouldn't they promote it?

Finally, I knew that arresting and deporting me would

bring enormous publicity, significantly increasing my audience.

I caught myself rubbing my hands together in glee.

I told the police that since the conference was over and it was no longer possible to give my talk, I wanted to leave Norway immediately. They seemed a bit surprised by this, probably because they are used to dealing with foreign freeloaders who will do anything to delay deportation.

I told them that I did not want to return to the United States. Instead, I wanted to go to Portugal, where I planned to attend an academic conference on immigration, multiculturalism, and the identitarian backlash. All I needed was my laptop to buy a ticket, my luggage, and a trip to the airport.

Unfortunately, as I was to learn, state deportation is far less efficient than self-deportation. I could have been on a plane that night. But they have rules. Following all those rules cost the Norwegian taxpayers a great deal of money and delayed my departure until the following Monday.

The letter they gave me also explained that I had the right to a state-appointed attorney. I told them I wanted to exercise that right to ensure that all my rights were respected and that I could be deported as quickly as possible.

I was returned to my cell and allowed to keep my glasses, so I could stare at a document in a language that I could not understand. The policemen went off to collect my baggage, both where I was staying and at the Scandza facility, a process that took many hours and multiple trips simply because I was not allowed to communicate with anyone.

After a couple of hours, I was summoned to speak to my attorney—or, as it turned out, the assistant to my attorney. I was introduced to a young woman who looked Persian or Kurdish. She told me she worked for Advocat Elden, which I assumed was the name of a law firm. I explained my desire to cooperate entirely and speed my departure. I also explained my desire to go to Portugal, not the United States. To my surprise, she seemed to indicate that her firm was already treating this as a free speech issue and that it was wrong to prevent me from speaking because of what other people might do. I didn't know what to make of this. I was entirely focused on getting out of there. I would think about a legal appeal once I was outside of Norwegian airspace.

The next morning, I was visited in my cell by a young woman with another letter stating the current disposition of my case. Again, it was read in English by an interpreter over a speakerphone. The letter mentioned the name of the lawyer I had spoken with the day before. It indicated that my request to self-deport had been received, as well as my preference to go to Portugal rather than return home. The letter explained in greater detail the rationale for my expulsion, which seemed to indicate that they were responding to arguments made by my lawyers. The letter ended by saying I would be deported immediately (meaning the next day), that I was not barred from returning to Norway in the future, that I had a three-week period for appeal, and that I could request to stay during the appeal. It did not seem to compute that I wanted to leave even *sooner* than "immediately" as they defined it. By "deporting" me, they were actually forcing me to stay in Norway longer.

The young woman also allowed me to call Fróði Midjord to assist in gathering the last of my belongings. But when he started telling me about what happened after my arrest, we were cut off.

Sunday afternoon, I was driven to a deportation "camp" near Oslo airport. After the indignity of a strip search, I was given my first hot meal. (Well, it had been hot an hour before. It seemed like jambalaya and chow mein cooked in the same pot. For almost a day and a half, I had been subsisting on bread, processed cheese slices, and milk.) Whereas previously, I had been locked in a cell, in the new facility, I had a private room but access to a common area. There were about eight other people awaiting deportation, all of them apparently Muslims. Although I was allowed to make phone calls, the computer system for that was down, so it was impossible.

Around seven in the evening, I was finally allowed to call my lawyer on one of the phones used by the staff. She explained that the state had now decided that I was free to go at any time. I could book a plane anywhere in the world that very evening. Unfortunately, it seemed to be too late to communicate this decision to the staff at the deportation facility, so I ended up taking the deportation flight out the next morning after another sleepless night.

Only after arriving at the airport was I given my phone. Nearly 48 hours had passed. Hundreds of messages began flooding into my various apps and email accounts. It was only then that I got a clear sense of the amazing things that had happened since my arrest.

Counter-Currents, November 6, 2019

The Oslo Incident[*]

Lana Lokteff: Welcome, ladies and gentlemen, because there's no in-between! Joining me is Greg Johnson, of *Counter-Currents*. He was detained, strip-searched, and deported from Norway. Why? For his thoughts!

Welcome thought criminal, political prisoner, and friend, Greg Johnson. How are you?

Greg Johnson: I'm fine. Thank you so much. This is the first interview I've given after my incarceration in Oslo this past weekend. I'm glad it's you. I am not giving any interviews to mainstream media people, because every one of them that has contacted me is from a network or platform that has used the slur "white supremacist" to describe me. If they can't respect my designated nouns, then I'm not going to give them any fresh quotes to decorate their boilerplate and help them support their narratives. So screw them! You're the first.

LL: Awesome! I love it.

GJ: We have our own media now.

LL: Yes, we do. Of course! I hate when people talk to the lame-stream. So, let's just back up a little bit. You went to beautiful Norway to give a talk at the Scandza Forum on "The Very Idea of White Privilege." Instead, you were arrested. I guess we can say detained, and then deported from Norway.

So, let's start from the beginning; and tell us the story.

GJ: I came to Oslo. This was my second time in Nor-

---

[*] This is a heavily edited transcript of my interview for Red Ice on November 7, 2019. I wish to thank Lana Lokteff for the interview and Hyacinth Bouquet for the transcript.

way. The first time I was there was in late June/early July of 2017, for the first Scandza Forum conference in Norway. It was the first event of its kind in Norway, and our friends in Norway wanted another conference. They wanted me to come back. So Fróði Midjord, who runs Scandza Forum, organized this event.

The theme of the conference was human biodiversity. With the exception of Fróði, who is the MC of the whole thing, all the speakers had Ph.D.s. There was me; there was Edward Dutton, who edits *Mankind Quarterly*; there were Kevin MacDonald and Helmuth Nyborg, both of whom are emeritus professors of psychology.

I was going to talk specifically about the idea of "white privilege." There are biological differences between the races and sexes that lead to different outcomes in society—even if everything is "fair." Even if the same rules apply to everyone, biological diversity creates different outcomes. When that happens, according to the PC mentality, that is a sign that something is wrong with society that has to be fixed. People are thinking wrong thoughts; institutions are wrong; unfairness is afoot.

Even though all kinds of explicit forms unfairness have been removed, we still find different outcomes. So they have increasingly "occult" explanations of different outcomes. The notion of "white privilege" is basically an odorless, colorless gas that pervades white societies and somehow keeps certain minority groups poor and in trouble with the law—more than average white people.

I argue that we can explain these different outcomes in terms of immutable biological differences. But I also argue that there is a legitimate sense of "white privilege." Because if groups really are different, then it stands to reason that groups will construct societies that reflect their natures. That means that other groups, if they try to enter these societies and make them multicultural, are going to find that they are not good fits. They're going to feel alienated, and they're going to think that the white people in these societies have all kinds of advantages.

And they do! Because the societies white people create are tailored to be comfortable to them, and that is a legitimate sense of "white privilege." But it's ultimately based on biology, and we have nothing to apologize for.

I was amazed, I was appalled, and I was very amused to find out that people in the Norwegian government, without knowing the topic or even the title of my talk, had become convinced that if I were allowed to speak, this would foment Right-wing terrorism in Norway. So I had to be arrested and expelled from the country.

I arrived at about 10:00 in the morning at the Scandza event facility. I was hanging out with friends. I met some new people. I was having a nice time. Not an hour went by before I was told by Fróði, "The police are here. They're coming to arrest you!" I thought, "Uh-oh!"

It wasn't entirely a surprise, because two days before, on Halloween, the day I arrived in Norway, we learned that *Filter News*, a Hope Not Hate/antifa-type blog, had run a piece on me, which I had to Google translate out of Norwegian. It claimed that I was an Anders Behring Breivik supporter, that I had claimed that his attacks were justified. It's all nonsense.

LL: It's all lies. Were there any sources in it? Of course not, because they can't prove any of that.

GJ: Well, there were sources that they quoted out of context. When they said that I said that Breivik's crimes were "necessary," I was talking about Breivik's *rationale* for why his crimes were necessary. They were ascribing his views to me. Anybody who read what I wrote on Breivik, honestly and intelligently, could not have concluded that. It was just a lie. It was just an attempt to smear me.

Later that day, another article appeared, created by the same Norwegian, communist soy-men. They had talked to one of their buddies, who is a terrorism researcher, and got a quote from him saying, "I think this guy needs to be barred from entering the country." Fróði said, "We need to prepare a response to this."

We went back and forth on Signal, drafting out a response. I said, "Okay. Translate this into Norwegian, tomorrow, Friday. If this attack has any traction, we will release it to the press. We will put it out on *Counter-Currents*. We will contact the press, if any of the mainstream news outlets in Norway take up this story." I was hoping it would just die out in the weeds, on the Left-wing fringe of the Norwegian internet, and that would be the end of it.

Friday was quiet. There really wasn't much to worry about, so I went about my business. I put finishing touches on my talk. I went out to dinner with the speakers and some friends.

The next morning, I arrived at the event venue and was informed that I was about to be arrested. I went outside, and there were two cops. I said, "Am I under arrest?" And they said, "Yes." I said, "What am I being arrested for?" They said they couldn't tell me. That sounded very irregular to me. I didn't know what Norwegian law is, though. It certainly would have been irregular in the United States. But I just went along with them. I figured, well, we'll see if we can clear this up quickly, so I said, "Let's go."

LL: Did they handcuff you?

GJ: No, nothing like that. It was super casual and polite. It was what you'd expect in a Nordic social democracy—kind of laid back.

LL: Where did they take you? Walk us through that whole experience.

GJ: They took me to a sort of non-descript part of the city, a diverse, immigrant-type neighborhood, with shawarma shops and graffiti everywhere, including hammer and sickles and antifa graffiti. It was a dump, a place where obviously nobody who lived there felt at home. There were some hipsters out walking tiny dogs. Bearded men, well dressed, with big flamboyant scarves, walking tiny dogs past graffiti saying, "Fuck hipsters," in English for some reason. I don't know why English is the international language of graffiti.

The booking process was Kafkaesque. They took my phone; they took my eyeglasses, my belt, my scarf, my coat, my shoes—anything that could be used as a weapon. Of course I was happy to surrender anything that could be plausibly used to kill me, thinking the worst-case scenario, of course, is Jeffrey Epstein, who didn't kill himself in jail. I figured I could work this out. I knew I had people on the outside who'd be concerned and would go to work on my behalf immediately. I was fully checked in by noon.

Once I was in my cell, there was no place to sit comfortably, so the only thing to do was to lie down. I tried to sleep. It's impossible to sleep in these jails. I was in a cell with no pillow, with a hard, plastic mattress and a blanket, which I wadded up into a pillow form. I was so uncomfortable that it was really impossible to sleep. I just physically ached.

So I started thinking about various possible outcomes. I came up with a list of possible outcomes, ranging from everything's okay and they'll allow me to leave, to Jeffrey Epstein. Then I isolated the ones that were most likely. Then I went through each likely outcome and tried to rank it in terms of likelihood. I tried to think of all the possible ins and outs. Then I tried to figure out how I could turn every outcome to my advantage and bounce back.

After a couple of hours pondering these things with my eyes closed, a thought came to my head: "Where are my feelings?" Because I wasn't feeling afraid. I wasn't feeling angry. I was just cold. I just felt cold and calm and calculating.

I spent a huge amount of time just meditating on different possibilities. I couldn't write anything down. You couldn't have pens or paper. I couldn't have a book. It's the kind of situation that can drive a person like me mad, but I tried to create a mental filing system so I could remember all these things.

I was not depressed at all. I managed to maintain good spirits throughout. Even though I was physically uncomfortable, I just said, "This is worth it. What I'm doing is meaningful. It's for Europa." And there are lots of people who have suffered far, far worse for the truth than I was. So I had to keep that in perspective.

LL: Were there other people around? Could you see other prisoners?

GJ: I couldn't see anyone. I could hear them. These places are all tile and concrete and really echoey. People would be whistling; they would be shouting; they'd be making noise; some of them sounded quite nuts.

You could hear every time a toilet flushed. It would rumble through the whole place. I know why people go mad in these sorts of environments. There is so much noise. You can't rest. You can't sleep at night, because people are peeking in to make sure you haven't offed yourself, and the last guy peeked in an hour before. I tried to sleep when I could. I don't think I slept more than three hours in the first 24 hours or more that I was there. They don't turn out the lights at night, either, which makes it hard to sleep.

That morning I'd had some coffee. I'd gotten Norwegian scones, which are distinct from other scones because they cost at least five dollars apiece. That's the only difference. They're just ridiculously expensive. I'd gotten a little bag of Norwegian scones for ten bucks, and I had nibbled my way through about a third of one scone before I was arrested.

So, I hadn't had any food yet. After several hours, I said, "Uh, I'm hungry." And so they handed me three slices of bread and three packages of processed cheese. I thought this was a snack. But no, that's all they gave me. I asked for more, and they brought me the same thing, plus little cartons of milk.

They seemed to have an unwritten rule, that no matter how simple your request is, they would count to one million—very slowly—before they would grant the request. It just took forever for the simplest things to happen.

It was several hours before I saw anybody. A young woman working for the immigration service asked me a few questions. She asked me how much money I had on me. She asked me about my passport, travel plans, stuff like that. It seemed to me that she was looking for an excuse to deport me. A pretext. For instance, I didn't have enough money for the time that I was going to stay in the country, or whatever.

I just answered the questions honestly. There was no point in lying. I didn't want to say, "I want to talk to a lawyer," at the time because I wasn't sure if I'd even really been arrested, what my status was, if I could call for a lawyer. She just jotted things down on a post-it note. It was very informal.

Then I talked to two plain-clothes cops. They have what I call the "Norwegian face." They looked like they could be cousins! There's a certain Norwegian look. They dressed like a lot of plain-clothes cops in America, kind of slovenly, to blend in, I guess, with the crowd. They were obviously very bright guys. They gave me a letter in Norwegian explaining what the state wanted to do. Then a woman who was an interpreter read it over the phone to me in English.

Basically, they told me that I was being detained and

that I would be deported under a provision of the Immigration Act, which allows aliens to be detained and deported for reasons of state or foreign policy. They specifically said that they believed if I were allowed to speak, I would foment Right-wing violence.

They didn't know the topic or title of my speech, but they somehow divined that it was going to cause violence. I was appalled by that. I kind of laughed at it. I tried not to be a jerk, because I wanted to be diplomatic, but inside, I was LOLing.

Moreover, if they had even bothered to look at what I had said at other Scandza Forums, for instance the very last Scandza Forum speech that I'd given, in Stockholm that year . . .

LL: It was against Right-wing terrorism, right?

GJ: Exactly. I'm the kind of guy who gets up and gives speeches that are designed to decrease the amount of Right-wing terrorism. And they're saying that if I spoke on "white privilege" it would have just the opposite effect.

I immediately knew what happened. Somebody in the Norwegian security apparatus had been "gotten to" by these antifa liars and had not even checked out the veracity of their claims. If they had simply read the articles by me—and I think they were actually live-linked in the piece—they would have seen that I was the victim of dishonest, out of context smearing. And they wouldn't have embarrassed themselves.

Either they were in on it—they were part of the communist, antifa, ultra-Left network in that country and doing a good deed for their comrades—or they were totally incompetent. Neither option is really a good look for the Norwegian Security Services. You want the intelligence apparatus in your country to be intelligent. You want the security service to actually make you more secure. You're not secure if you have people who are dishonest, or just incompetent, making decisions like this.

I thought, well, this could be interesting. We could sue these "journalists" for libel. I wanted to look into that. I wanted to look into whether or not the whole thing could be overturned if we could prove that it was based on a libel. But the first thing I wanted to do was just get the hell out of Norway! It was after five, so I said, "The time of my lecture has passed. The event is basically over."

LL: So, "Let me go."

GJ: "Let me go!" I want to deport myself. I want to get out of the country that night. I said, "Just bring me my laptop. I'll buy a ticket. I'll gather my bags, and I'll be out of your hair." They were a little taken aback by that because they're used to people who want to stay and freeload off the system as long as possible. I just wanted to go.

LL: Can you choose where you're being deported? Can you choose which country you want to go to, or do you have to go back to the country you're from?

GJ: You have to go back where you're from. And that was not my first choice, because I was planning to spend several days in Lisbon. I was going to go to an academic conference at the university, where they had various scholars of identitarianism, the Alt Right, etc.: people like Eric Kaufmann, Angela Nagle, and George Hawley. It was an academic conference on immigration, multiculturalism, and the identitarian backlash. It was open to the public, and I wanted to go. I wanted to meet these people. I wanted to listen to their talks, maybe ask a couple of questions, use it as an opportunity for dialogue. I wanted to go there immediately. I didn't want to stick around any longer because I had no reason to stay.

I also made a very good decision. The letter said that I had the right to an attorney, and to have an attorney appointed to me. I said, "I want to exercise my right to an attorney. I want to leave as soon as possible. Before you can deport me, I want to be gone. But I want to make sure that my rights are not violated and to expedite this process as much as possible."

They called an attorney, and they started trying to gather my stuff. There was some stuff at the place I was staying, some stuff at Scandza. Of course, I couldn't get on the phone and just call people. I had to tell them where things were. And, of course, they would go to places and pick things up; but they wouldn't pick up certain things, because they didn't know if they were mine. It just went on and on. It was a lesson in how self-deportation is much more efficient than being deported by the state. If they had just given me my phone, I would have been out of there! Just drive me to the airport; that's all you need to do. It took them two days.

So after about two hours of waiting, I again was ushered into a room. There was a woman who was my lawyer. She appeared to be Iranian, maybe Kurdish.

LL: I'm sure they love that. Let's see his face when he sees her, right? But it turns out she was pro free speech, right?

GJ: Totally. She said she worked for "Advocat Eldin." I thought that could be the name of a company, like a law firm. I don't know Norwegian. Maybe it was free legal aid, for all I knew.

Anyway, she was really nice. I just explained to her that I wanted to go as quickly as possible, but I wanted to make sure my rights were respected. She said, "We'll do what we can. I'll get in touch with the firm." I realized she was the assistant to another lawyer. She also said at this point they'd already filed a free speech complaint. She said, "We want you to know that we don't think you've done anything wrong, and it is wrong for them to detain you and prevent you from speaking because of what somebody *might* do if you're allowed to speak." What *somebody else* might do. It is an absurd situation that you can be arrested for what other people *might* do. It turned out that the whole country was talking about my case. It was the number one news item. Even people on the Left thought it outrageous.

LL: Well, here they were happy about it. All of a sudden, lefties here in America, they love hardcore borders and deportation of people in Europe. They love it in your case, of course.

GJ: I know, exactly. These globalists have one principle, which is to destroy us. That governs everything. They are all for open borders when it means Muslims and Third Worlders coming in, and they are all for sovereignty and deportation and Schengen bans when it keeps *us* from moving around.

LL: Keeping white people out of Europe.

GJ: Keeping white people out of Europe. Keeping people from meeting face-to-face. They're willing to use national sovereignty and deportation law to further the globalist cause, which will eventually abolish all of these things.

At the time, I was so focused on getting out of there I didn't ask her any questions about the free speech angle. I figured I'll just deal with that later, if at all. I just wanted to get out of Norway and on to my next destination.

Later that night, I met another plain-clothes cop, who was clearly dressed to blend in with an antifa crowd, a very dignified man with greying hair and beard. He told me that 28 people had been arrested. Protestors had been at the forum. They'd been told to disperse and had been arrested.

He was trying to locate some of my luggage that was at the forum site. They took very seriously my desire to self-deport and tried to get my stuff for me. I appreciated that. I honestly thought they were being sincere and doing their level best. They thought, "This is the easiest case that has come along in a long time. He just wants to go." I'm sure they're constantly dealing with people who are delaying the whole process.

The next day, a young woman who worked for the Norwegian immigration police came to my cell with a new letter. Another woman read it in English over the phone. It was apparent that the lawyer had been at work because her name was mentioned in it.

Basically, they were responding to the free speech objections to my arrest. I thought it interesting that they were trying to actually justify their position. But they didn't justify the underlying assumptions that I was a Breivik apologist and that by speaking I would produce more Breiviks. The lawyer didn't know to question it. I didn't really focus on that when I talked to her.

I was told that I would be deported. They seemed to be open about the destination. I was hoping that they would let me go to Portugal rather than send me home. It seemed like things were budging. It seemed like there was some back and forth, there was some discussion going on, and their position was loosening up a bit. I thought that was interesting.

Later that day, I was transferred to another facility, a camp near the airport for deportation. I had to go through the whole process of being fingerprinted again. I had the indignity of a strip search. It was humiliating—for them. Then I got my first hot meal. I was given my own room with a private bathroom. It was much more comfortable. There was also a common area where you could get coffee, juice, etc. I was getting dehydrated, so I got a couple of giant cartons of apple juice and drank them. I could just take anything I wanted. They only locked us in our rooms at night.

I tried to make phone calls. I was told I could, but the system was down. Eventually, around seven at night, I spoke to my lawyer who told me that the authorities had decided I was free to go. I could go to the airport and book any flight out to anywhere in the world. Or I could stay for the period of my appeal. Or I could get on the deportation flight the next morning.

I said, "Great, I want to go. Can you get on the phone to the people who run this facility, explain to them the change in plans, have them give me my access to a computer? I'll see if I can book a flight." But it was too late. Nobody was there who could process my release. I just had to go to bed, another sleepless night.

I took the deportation flight because that was the most practical option at that point. It was a rather pleasant experience. When Freud was expelled from Austria by the Nazis, he was asked to sign a document stating that he had not been mistreated. He wrote, as if he were reviewing a hotel, "I can heartily recommend the Gestapo to anyone." I always loved that. I can heartily recommend being deported from Norway to anyone. It's the best air travel experience I've ever had.

Two cops picked me up. They were nice guys. They shook my hand. Everything was very friendly and cordial. They got my bags and took me to the airport. They said, "Okay, we're going through security." There was no line. It was just a tiny private security area, for staff people to go through. It took minutes.

Then they took me to a lounge, where I was the only person. There was a really good coffee machine there, so I had my first coffee in a couple days. They had free food: Ramen noodles, stuff like that. I just skipped it. I was hoping I could go to the regular airport terminal, where I could buy some five-dollar scones. That wasn't an option.

They gave me my phone back. I had been incommunicado almost 48 hours at that point, except for one brief call to Fróði about my bags, which they cut off when we started trying to talk about what had actually happened at the Scandza event. So this was my first real contact with the world. I turned the phone on and watched as hundreds of messages downloaded. Friends all over the world were frantically worried.

Then I called Fróði, and he said, "It's amazing! We're the number one news item for two days in a row. When you requested a lawyer, John Christian Elden—who's the best-known lawyer in the country—stepped forward and is representing you." That was the "Advocat Elden" the woman worked for. He was Varg Vikernes's lawyer at one time. I thought, "This is an amazing stroke of luck."

Folks, if you're ever in trouble with the law, ask for a lawyer. You could luck out and get the number one lawyer in the country. Elden was probably circling, salivating for the chance to represent me because he likes free speech cases and high-profile cases, and this was a big news event.

I spent about 45 minutes sipping coffee, talking to Fróði, reading messages, and realizing what an amazing weekend the rest of the world had had while I'd been incommunicado. Then it was time to go. The police drove me to the airplane; they drove me across the tarmac to the base of the gangway tower. We went up a little staircase to the entry gangway. There was a yellow ribbon across the opening of the plane, saying "Don't Enter." The plane was not open yet. I was going to be the first passenger on the plane.

At this point I was sending my first tweet, "I'm free! And Jeffrey Epstein still did not kill himself!" I sent it, and the two cops were wondering why I was chuckling. I said, "Apparently, I'm some kind of celebrity." Of course they knew, because they had been following the news the whole weekend. Everybody knew. But I didn't know that they knew, because they were all being very professional, and I appreciated that.

The pilot or the co-pilot came down the gangway to the plane, and I shook his hand. He smiled. Obviously, he knew who I was. I thought, "Gee, this is great! This is total V.I.P. treatment."

A stewardess opened the plane up. I was the first passenger on the plane. I sat down, got comfortable, and put on my dark glasses to hide from paparazzi. Then I tried to prop my eyelids open with toothpicks and start writing! I could write now. I finally had a pen and paper. I started writing out an account of everything that happened.

The hilarious thing was that I wasn't technically deported. I could have left any time, or I could have stayed, but I chose to get on the flight that they had paid for and be deported, because it was the most practical option. Honestly, at that point I was so exhausted that the idea of spending several days in Lisbon at a conference, sleeping in a strange bed, was not appealing. I decided it was just best to go home. I needed to sleep, communicate with my lawyer, write up an account of what happened, and also deal with requests for interviews.

It was easy to eliminate most interviews. I refused to talk to anybody who used the "white supremacist" slur. There have got to be consequences for that kind of dishonest and lazy journalism. We have our own media, and I don't need these people. They need us more than we need them, at this point.

There is a horrible movie called *The Human Centipede*. I won't elaborate on it. You can Google it. That's my image of the mainstream media. They feed on one another's lies and hysteria. Their job is deception.

Before I actually saw myself in the funhouse mirror of the mainstream media, I used to think that people who get attacked in the media must have done something wrong. Where there's smoke, there's fire, right? But when you know the truth about yourself and see just how systematically everything is distorted—even simple things, even things that there's no advantage to distorting—it's very sobering. When I was in graduate school, one of my professors compared grading papers to fever dreams, in which one's daily activities come back in garbled form. That's the experience you have when you see yourself discussed by media people.

LL: Why you? Why are you such a threat?

GJ: That's a good question. Why didn't they target Kevin MacDonald? He was there too, and he's a far more important person than I am. I don't know why they targeted me, not him. They even found Kevin making comments about Breivik. They said, "Oh! He's another Breivik supporter." But they didn't try to arrest and expel him. Maybe they think I'm going good work. Maybe they think that I should be taken down a peg. Certainly, the amount of repression and deplatforming that we are facing has been ratcheted up enormously.

If that was their goal, they failed miserably. The whole incident enormously increased my visibility and *Counter-Currents'* traffic, not just in Norway but around the world. I knew it would happen. As I sat in that office with the plain-clothes cops, listening to the interpreter translate the letter about what was happening, I found myself gleefully rubbing my hands together. That's probably a hate crime in Norway.

By preventing me from speaking to a gathering of 90 people, they gave me press coverage allowing millions of people to hear about me. What a dumb move on their part! If they wanted my ideas to remain marginal and obscure, they should have just ignored me and let me go about my business, and that would have been that.

Thanks to my arrest, I was the number one story in Norway for two days running. That weekend, our traffic was up about 30 or 40 percent. The month before my arrest, Norway was our number 16 country in terms of traffic. Norway has four million people. But it's in our top twenty, which means that a significant percentage of Norwegians are reading the site. More Norwegians in a country of four million are reading our site than Brazilians in a country of tens of millions. That's interesting. This month Norway is number four. So they jumped from sixteenth to fourth in terms of countries reading our site. They're ahead of Germany, France, Australia, Canada, all much bigger countries.

LL: Weren't you blocked from speaking at the Copenhagen Scandza Forum? What happened there?

GJ: Three weeks to the day before the event in Oslo, we had a Scandza Forum in Copenhagen. I got there about thirty minutes before the event was supposed to start, and there was a huge mob of black-clad antifa—I'd say sixty to eighty people—besieging the building. They were actually carrying the flag of the Soviet Union. The flag that flew over the Gulag!

These people are communists. No, they're not "the real fascists"! They are actual communists. One of these people, a six-foot-four freak with a nose ring, had the hammer and sickle tattooed on his forehead and a Kalashnikov tattooed on his check. These people are advertising what they are. But a lot of normies won't accept the message.

The police created a perimeter around the Antifa, but they didn't clear them away to allow conference attendees to safely enter the building. This was just dereliction on the part of the police. So I couldn't get in. About a third of the attendees couldn't get in the facility. Most of the talks did happen. The videos of them are up on the Scandza channel.

It wasn't all bad. I bumped into a couple of people that I knew. There were a couple of people that I planned to meet at the event, and I bumped into them outside. Since we couldn't get in, we spent the day talking. I met Laura Towler and hung out with her. There was a core group of four who went through the whole experience together. But there were antifa lurking in the neighborhood too. Finally, around 4:30, I decided to just give up and head back to my hotel.

Because of my experience in Copenhagen, I went to the Oslo event two hours early, thinking that if there were a siege, at least I'd be inside, not anticipating that I would be taken away by the cops before the event could begin. The antifa came; they protested; they cut the power at one point. But the event went on. The police did their jobs. They cleared them away. Only three people didn't show up, and they might not have been kept away by antifa. One of them might have been an antifa mole, for all we know. All the speeches but mine were delivered and videoed. They also videoed the mayhem outside. Twenty-eight protesters were arrested and have been hit with huge fines by the government. This is very, very encouraging.

After the events in Copenhagen, mainstream papers were decrying antifa violence. These counties are surprisingly sensible. Sweden is the nuttiest country in Scandinavia. The Danes are probably the most sober-minded. Norway quietly decided in recent years to back slowly away from the abyss; they seem to be inching towards Danish rather than Swedish attitudes.

The public in Scandinavia is pro-free speech, which is good. In Denmark, in the last elections, Mette Frederiksen of the Social Democrats ran on an anti-immigration, anti-globalization platform. Her position was that globalization and immigration are bad for Danish workers, the constituency that Social Democrats need to take care of. Instead of debating whether or not immigration is a good thing, now the real debate in Denmark is how re-migrate them back to their homelands. That's enormous progress, metapolitically speaking.

When asked the question, "What are your feelings about Denmark's reputation as an Islamophobic country?" I think about 15 percent of Danes said they were ashamed of that, and more than 70 percent said they were perfectly comfortable with that. The rest didn't know. That's very encouraging. Mette Frederiksen said, "Being opposed to immigration doesn't make you a bad person." That is a huge metapolitical gain for us. When people get over the idea that nationalism is immoral, everything is possible.

When I was locked up, I was rehearsing answers to hostile questions from the press. I was thinking: What if they throw the "Nazi" question at me? "Do you believe in National Socialism?" or something like that. My answer would have been: "Absolutely not. I believe in Nordic social democracy without multiculturalism." If you put it that way, most people in Nordic countries would probably think, at least privately, "Yes. Why not? Why not Nordic social democracy without all these problems that we've been importing?"

LL: I have to ask you: How far are you willing to go? If they really clamp down, they're coming for you, how deep are you going to go into this?

GJ: For me, there is no exit. There is no backing out. We just have to go deeper, deeper into the struggle until we come out the other side. Until we have victory.

LL: Ultimately, take it as a compliment; and hopefully it's inspiring for you to continue. I've already said, we're going to do what we need to. If we need to go back to living in a studio apartment, if we have to do what we're going to do, we're not going to quit.

GJ: It's worth it. Somebody has to do this. I *enjoy* doing this. I have a meaningful life. I have traveled to interesting places. I have met fascinating people. I've even been to jail! I'm looking forward to writing my memoirs. I'm doing something meaningful and effective. I think that's why I'm being persecuted. And I'm just going to keep doing it until we win.

Counter-Currents, April 7, 2021

THE NORWEGIAN SECRET POLICE'S ORDER TO DETAIN GREG JOHNSON

On November 2, 2019, I was detained by Norwegian police on the orders of the Norwegian Police Security Service (Politiets Sikkerhetstjeneste, PST) to prevent me from delivering a lecture at the Scandza Forum in Oslo.

Norwegian journalists investigating my detention have requested access to the PST's letter explaining their rationale for my arrest. Their requests have been denied on the grounds that the document is "classified."

However, it is my right under Norwegian law to see this document, and it is also my right to make it public, which I am doing below. I have made only one alteration to this letter. I have removed the name and signature of the responsible officer, lest I be accused of some form of harassment.

The letter is followed by a translation into English (with thanks to Fróði Midjord) as well as my commentary showing that the PST simply copied the rationale for my arrest from a Left-extremist (antifa) blog that was openly trying to sabotage the Scandza Forum. Furthermore, the PST clearly failed to make even the most cursory attempt to verify the claims of such a biased source.

Finally, I point out that in addition to the frankly laughable claim that my speech at Scandza was likely to promote political violence, the PST makes it abundantly clear that their aim is *simply to suppress freedom of speech and thought about alternative political ideas in Norway*, and they are doing so at the behest of unelected and unaccountable Left-wing extremists.

Unntatt offentlighet jf
offentleglova § 13

POLITIETS
SIKKERHETSTJENESTE

Postboks 4773 Nydalen
0421 OSLO

Utlendingsdirektoratet (UDI)

ANMODNING OM VURDERING AV BORTVISNING

Saken gjelder: Greg JOHNSON, borger av USA, fødselsdato ukjent.

Det vises til telefonsamtale tidligere i dag.

PST har opplysninger om at ovennevnte kan komme reisende til Oslo lufthavn, Gardermoen i dag.

Greg JOHNSON er ifølge åpne kilder annonsert som en av talerne på Scandza Forum som avholdes på et hemmelig sted i Oslo 02.11.2019.

Greg JOHNSON er en av frontfigurene i et nettverk av skribenter og foredragsholdere som forfekter jødehat og raseteorier, samt hvit nasjonalisme. I invitasjonen til Scandza forum sin konferanse 1. juli 2017 ble han omtalt som «en av de ledende ideologene innenfor den hvite nasjonalistiske bevegelsen». Han er blant annet redaktør i den nettbaserte alt-right publikasjonen Counter-Currents.

JOHNSON har tidligere uttrykt støtte til hvordan Anders BREIVIK begrunnet 22 juli-angrepet, og har referert til terroren som *nødvendig*. JOHNSON skal også ha skrevet en artikkel i etterkant av rettsaken mot BREIVIK hvor han beskriver sin nyvunne «respekt» for massedrapsmannen, som han mente hadde «agert ut fra lojaliteten til sitt folk». Videre beskriver JOHNSON at BREIVIK «har fremstått på en verdig måte og hare kommet med et kraftfullt intelligent og vel argumentert forsvar av sitt syn og handlinger.»

I en tekst publisert 18. mai 2012 skal JOHNSON ha skrevet: «*Det norske arbeiderparti er ansvarlig for all volden forårsaket av dere politikk, inkludert den uunngåelige volden fra nordmenn som gikk lei og endelig slo tilbake*».

Scandza-forum er et internasjonalt nettverk av høyreekstreme som jevnlig arrangerer samlinger i Norden. Tidligere samlinger i 2018-19 har tiltrukket seg 50-200 deltakere, hvorav flere har vært kjente høyreekstreme. Til møtene inviteres høyreekstreme ideologer fra USA og Europa som foredragsholdere.

Side 1 av 2

Side 2 av 2

PST vurderer det som sannsynlig at det ideologiske budskapet som formidles under disse samlingene kan inspirere deltakerne til utøvelse av politisk motivert vold.

PST er bekymret for at JOHNSON gjennom å delta på en konferanse i regi av Scandza forum vil være med å bidra til økt radikalisering, inspirere til utøvelse av politisk motivert vold, samt bidra at alt-right/identitær-miljøet skal få et sterkere fotfeste i Norge.

Det er PSTs vurdering at ovennevnte person representerer en trussel mot grunnleggende nasjonale interesser og at vilkårene for bortvisning etter utlendingsloven § 126 annet ledd er oppfylt. Det er PSTs vurdering at dersom han får gjennomført det planlagte foredraget, eventuelle etterfølgende møter eller andre tilsvarende arenaer/møteplasser, vil det kunne bidra til å inspirere eller motivere til ekstremistiske handlinger og holdninger.

Det anmodes om at UDI vurderer om vilkårene er oppfylt for å treffe vedtak om bortvisning fra riket med hjemmel i utlendingsloven § 126 første ledd annet punktum.

Politiets sikkerhetstjeneste, 01.november 2019

Fung sjef PST

ENGLISH TRANSLATION

From:
POLICE SECURITY SERVICE
PO Box 4773 Nydalen
0421 OSLO

To:
Directorate of Immigration (UDI)

RE: REQUEST FOR REVIEW OF DEPORTATION

The case is: Greg JOHNSON, US citizen, date of birth unknown.

In reference to the phone call earlier today.

PST has information that the above may travel to Oslo Gardermoen Airport today.

According to public sources, Greg JOHNSON has been announced as one of the speakers at the Scandza Forum, which is being held in a secret location in Oslo on 02.11.2019.

Greg JOHNSON is one of the front men in a network of writers and lecturers who advocate Jew-hatred and racial theories, as well as White Nationalism. In the invitation to Scandza Forum's conference on July 1, 2017, he was referred to as "One of the leading ideologues in the White Nationalist movement." He is, among other things, the editor of the online Alt-Right publication *Counter-Currents*.

JOHNSON has previously expressed support for how Anders BREIVIK justified the July 22 attack, and has referred to the terror as "necessary." JOHNSON also wrote an article following the BREIVIK trial describing his newfound "respect" for the mass murderer, who he believed had "acted out of loyalty to his people." JOHNSON further describes that BREIVIK "comported himself in a dignified manner and made a forceful, intelligent, well-argued case for his views and actions."

In a text published on May 18, 2012, JOHNSON supposedly wrote: "The Norwegian Labor Party is responsible for all of the violence caused by their policies, including the inevitable violence by Norwegians who get fed up and finally fight back."

The Scandza Forum is an international network of Right-wing extremists who regularly hold gatherings in the Nordic countries. Previous meetings in 2018–19 have attracted 50–200 participants, several of whom have been well-known Right-wing extremists. Right-wing ideologues from the US and Europe are invited to speak at the meetings.

The PST considers it likely that the ideological message conveyed during these meetings may inspire the participants to engage in politically motivated violence.

PST is concerned that JOHNSON, through attending a conference organized by the Scandza Forum, will help contribute to increased radicalization, inspiring engagement in politically motivated violence, and help give the Alt-Right/Identitarian milieu a stronger foothold in Norway.

It is PST's assessment that the above person represents a threat to basic national interests and that the conditions for expulsion pursuant to section 126, second paragraph, of the Immigration Act are fulfilled. It is the opinion of the PST that if he carries out the planned lecture, any possible subsequent meetings, or other similar gatherings, it could help inspire or motivate extremist actions and attitudes.

It is requested that the UDI [Directorate of Immigration] assess whether the conditions are fulfilled in order to make a decision on expulsion from the state on the basis of § 126, first paragraph, second sentence, of the Immigration Act.

Police Security Service, November 01, 2019

COMMENTS BY GREG JOHNSON

The Norwegian Police Security Service (PST) letter of November 1, 2019 supporting my detention and expulsion from Norway is disturbing for three main reasons. First, I was detained and deported based on false information that the PST never bothered to check. Second, the main charge against me—that I am an apologist for terrorism—is a complete inversion of the truth, and a highly damaging one. Finally, the letter clearly indicates that I was expelled not simply because of the (wholly spurious) threat of political violence, but because the PST seeks to suppress national populist ("Alt Right" and "Identitarian") political ideas in Norway.

The case for my detention and expulsion was based on a couple of blog posts written by Harald S. Kungtveit and Jonas Skybakmoen on October 31st on *Filter Nyheter*, a Left-wing extremist ("antifa") blog. As I argue at length in my essay "Anarcho-Tyranny in Oslo," reprinted above, these articles are deeply dishonest, quoting passages and single words of my essay "Breivik: A Strange New Respect"[1] out of context to argue for a complete inversion of my meaning.

The PST's letter, for example, copies the *Filter Nyheter's* claim that I regarded Breivik's terrorism as "necessary," whereas taken in context it is clear that I am simply referring to Breivik's own rationale for his terrorism.

The PST's letter also copies *Filter Nyheter* in stating that after Breivik's trial, I had a newfound "respect" for him, ignoring the facts that (1) "respect" is a relative term, and prior to his trial I had expressed utmost contempt for

---

[1] Greg Johnson, "Breivik: A Strange New Respect," *Confessions of a Reluctant Hater*.

Breivik (see my article "Anders Behring Breivik: The Neoconservative Rambo"[2]), so I had in effect raised him a few rungs in hell, (2) I concluded that Breivik still failed to make a compelling case for terrorism, even on his own terms, and (3) I offered my own powerful case against terrorism.

It is clear to me that the PST never checked the statements in *Filter Nyheter*. Whether it was out of collusion or simple incompetence needs to be determined.

Presumably, if the Norwegian PST thinks that I should be detained and deported to prevent me from giving a speech, they must think I am a highly persuasive individual. But if they had made even a cursory search to see *the sorts of things I actually say*, they would have learned that *I am famous in White Nationalist circles for condemning terrorism*. For instance, the last talk I delivered at a Scandza Forum meeting (Stockholm, March 30, 2019) was called "Against Right-Wing Terrorism" (reprinted below as "Against White Nationalist Terrorism"). Indeed, I have published more than a dozen articles over the years condemning Right-wing terrorism.[3]

If the PST is really interested in decreasing the likelihood of Right-wing terrorism, they should have welcomed me to Norway with a red carpet.

The PST argued that I be detained and deported because my speech was a threat to national security on three grounds: (1) that it "will help contribute to increased radicalization," (2) that it will inspire engagement in "politically motivated violence," and (3) that it will "help give the Alt-Right/Identitarian milieu a stronger foothold in Norway."

---

[2] Greg Johnson, "Anders Behring Breivik: The Neoconservative Rambo," *Confessions of a Reluctant Hater*.

[3] Listed in "Greg Johnson Arrested in Norway for Thoughtcrime," *Counter-Currents*, November 2, 2019.

First of all, I must point out the sheer absurdity that the PST somehow concluded that these outcomes were likely *without knowing the topic or even the title of my speech.* (My speech is called "The Very Idea of White Privilege." The topic of the conference was Human Biodiversity.)

Second, when one drops the wholly spurious claim that my speech represents a terrorist threat, all that remains is the transparent motive to use the power of the state to suppress free debate and free thought about political ideas. The PST is, in fact, acting as the Thought Police.

I have many readers and friends in Norway. I was invited to Norway to address them. I am appalled that the Norwegian state sent police to prevent me from speaking.

But it is especially galling that I was detained under false pretenses concocted by Left-extremists whose express purpose was shutting down the Scandza Forum.

The charge of being an apologist for terrorism is especially alarming, given that in today's world, people who are accused of terrorism are subject to extrajudicial imprisonment and torture, to say nothing of personal and professional damages.

It is deeply disturbing that such damaging charges from such suspect sources were not checked, as their falsehood could have been easily ascertained. This is a serious lapse of professional conduct and basic ethics. *In a free country, the state does not pass down momentous, life-changing judgments and dispatch armed police to prevent an individual from speaking based on unchecked assertions made by his political enemies.* This is the kind of behavior one associates with totalitarian states.

Counter-Currents, November 15, 2019

Against White Nationalist Terrorism*

White Nationalist terrorism—such as Brenton Tarrant's shooting spree in New Zealand and the similar crimes of Robert Bowers and Dylann Roof—hurts White Nationalism and helps our enemies in at least four ways.

- First, the goal of White Nationalism is to persuade whites that we are better off separating ourselves from non-whites. Terrorism, however, makes many whites feel sympathetic to the non-white victims. It makes white liberals want to hug them, dress like them, and further accommodate them—when we want them to do just the opposite. That's obviously self-defeating.
- Second, our job is to convince the world that White Nationalism is the solution to ethnic conflict, not a cause of it. White Nationalist terrorism undermines that message and is thus self-defeating as well.
- Third, White Nationalist terrorism energizes the Left. It gives them options for virtue signaling, manufacturing martyrs, and ginning up moral panics. Clearly, we have a better chance of beating the Left if they are enervated and demoralized, not energized and indignant.
- Fourth, these moral panics are used as pretexts for repressing White Nationalists, specif-

---

* Originally given under the title "Against Right-Wing Terrorism" at the Scandza Forum in Stockholm on March 30, 2019.

ically our freedom of speech and our right to bear arms. That too is obviously self-defeating.

Before one starts a fight, any smart combatant takes stock of his strengths and weaknesses, and the strengths and weaknesses of his enemy. So let's take stock.

Racially conscious white people lack numbers. We are a tiny minority. We lack money. We lack leadership and organization. We lack institutional power and influence. On the other hand, we do have truth, morality, and practical solutions on our side. We know that racial and ethnic diversity in the same society causes alienation, tension, hatred, and violence. We are also the only people offering a workable alternative: first, to stop increasing diversity; second, to restore or create racially and ethnically homogeneous homelands for all peoples.

Our strengths and weakness are the mirror image of the strengths and weaknesses of our enemies. The advocates of globalization and multiculturalism have numbers. They even have even convinced the vast majority of our own people—the primary victims of diversity—to take the side of our abusers and dispossessors. They have effectively unlimited money. They can just print it. They have leadership. All the political leaders, Left, Right, and center, are working for them. We have no political leaders who actually represent us. They also have control over the leading institutions of our society: academia, religion, business, and government, including the military and police.

But the establishment has some important disadvantages. First of all, globalization and multiculturalism are premised on falsehoods about what makes a society good. They are also premised on a false moral system that blames whites for things we did not do, and excuses non-whites for their real failings and offenses. They preach diversity for others but avoid it themselves, making them rank hypocrites. Because they are responsible for policies that are producing terrible consequences, they must lie to cover up the disasters they create and divert blame to the innocent. On top of that, they are corrupt, hysterical, degenerate, and downright silly.

So given these strengths and these weaknesses, on our side and on their side, where should we attack our enemies? Should we attack them where they're strongest or where they're weakest? And how should we attack them? From a position of strength or a position of weakness? The smartest strategy is to attack our enemies at their weakest from a position of strength. The dumbest strategy is to attack our enemies at their strongest from a position of weakness.

We can't beat them in democratic contests. We can't beat them in armed struggle. We can't outspend them. But we can out-argue them. We can out-meme them. We can shame and mock and humiliate them. Truth and morality are on our side. We have enormous advantages in the intellectual and cultural realm of struggle. So we should attack their weaknesses from our strengths.

A great example of such activism is the so-called Alt Right, the largely anonymous online network of White Nationalists and national populists that in 2015 and 2016 became the bane of mainstream conservatism and the most energetic supporters of Donald Trump. The Alt Right at its peak was a beautiful thing. It was an example of effective metapolitics in action. We were making genuine progress by changing people's minds. Indeed, the main reason the Left has been screaming for increased social media censorship and deplatforming is that they got tired of losing arguments with us.

But then our people got a little giddy and started memeing in real life. But as we discovered with the "Hailgate" fiasco, anonymous online memes—especially of the Nazi variety—didn't play well in the real world.

Then in 2017 there was a rash of public demonstrations and speeches, and we found that White Nationalists were not really able to stand up against the organized Left. Because even antifa, who are criminals, could count on the indulgence and secret support of the establishment. Every single one of the rioters that trashed Washington, D.C. at the Trump inauguration has been let off. It took a couple of years, but they've all gotten off. Meanwhile, people on the Right who defended themselves from antifa are having the book thrown at them. Our organizations are also being plagued and bankrupted by lawfare. And we simply don't have the resources to fight back.

In 2015 and 2016, we won enormous victories by attacking the enemy's weakest points from a position of strength. In 2017 we suffered enormous defeats because we thought we could attack our enemy's strongest points from a position of weakness. These defeats were entirely predictable, but the wrong people were making decisions.

Since then, the consensus has been to return to what worked: metapolitics, which includes community building, online propaganda, and Identitarian-style activism, which aims to maximize impacts on the public mind while minimizing risks and costs to activists. We can't outgun the enemy. We can't outspend them. But we can out-argue them. We can be cooler, cleverer, and funnier. We can change minds, and the establishment is powerless to change them back.

White Nationalists win every fair debate. Thus the longer White Nationalists can stay in the public sphere, the more minds we can change. The more minds we change, the greater the likelihood of restoring white homelands.

Every incident of lone-wolf White Nationalist terrorism, however, is used as an excuse for further censorship, deplatforming, and harassment of *all* White Nationalists, even those who have nothing to do with such crimes. Therefore, White Nationalist terrorism is counterproductive.

Fortunately, I do not think that our message can be completely suppressed, for two important reasons.

First, the establishment wants to believe that the only thing preventing the emergence of a global, multicultural utopia are skeptics like us, exercising our freedom of speech to persuade people that multiculturalism and globalization are bad things. But in truth the main factors driving the rise of white identity politics are the catastrophic consequences of multiculturalism and globalization themselves.

This means that even if the establishment could censor and deplatform us entirely, it wouldn't stop the rise of white identity politics. Because as hard as White Nationalists are working to raise our people's consciousness, we're not doing a fraction of the consciousness-raising that the establishment is by imposing multiculturalism and globalization. But it is still important to keep our voices heard, so we can deepen our people's understanding of the problems we face and offer them workable alternatives to the present system.

Second, the only way the establishment could censor and deplatform us completely is to shut down the internet, which is impossible because the world economic system has come to depend upon it.

But although censorship cannot stop us, it can surely slow us down, and every day that we are delayed will be paid for by white people who suffer and die—and white people who are never born—because we lack homelands of our own. Thus Brenton Tarrant did more than kill fifty Muslims in New Zealand. He killed uncounted white people by delaying the day we get our homelands back.

Now at this point, many people object: "But surely

you don't think we are going to *vote* our way out of this mess." My answer is simple. There are many ways we might create white homelands, including winning elections. But no matter how we end up establishing white homelands, we are going to need a lot more White Nationalists to do it. How do we create more White Nationalists? By converting people, i.e., by changing people's minds. Which leads us back to metapolitics.

Even if you think the only way to establish a white homeland is through revolution, the first step has to be propaganda. You will need to explain to people *what* White Nationalism is and *why* it is necessary, which is what all White Nationalists—no matter how we envision the path to victory—need to be doing. In addition to that, you will have to persuade people that revolution is the best way to establish white homelands. But even that is not enough. Then you will have to persuade people to join your revolution. And since you are more likely to win if more people sympathize with and fewer people resist your cause, you will need to persuade them as well.

So my recommendation to the advocates of revolution is to start persuading people.

Now ask yourself: What are the primary impediments to reaching and persuading the public? Clearly they are censorship and deplatforming. Now ask yourself: What is the most common pretext for censoring and deplatforming us? Clearly it is acts of violence, like Tarrant's rampage. So advocates of revolution—if they really are serious—need to discourage White Nationalist terrorism as much as the rest of us.

What can we do to stop White Nationalist terrorism? I can think of four things.

- ❖ First, we have to dismantle the intellectual case for terrorism, which is what I am doing right here.

- ❖ Second, we have to mock and shame the follies and vices that contribute to terrorism, including anti-intellectualism, unseriousness, juvenile LARPing and bloody-mindedness, nihilism, macho posturing, paranoia and pessimism, and apocalyptic all-or-nothing thinking.
- ❖ Third, we have to ban all people who call for violence from our websites, meetings, and organizations.
- ❖ Fourth, if someone comes to us making credible threats of terrorism, we need to be the ones to call the police.

This last suggestion has proved controversial. After all, the police do not have a sterling record of honorable dealings with nationalists. But even if the police are unworthy of contact, that does not imply that people like Brenton Tarrant or Robert Bowers are worthy of our silence. After all, they are doing objective harm to our cause. Indeed, Tarrant's explicit goal was to provoke a crackdown on white advocates to make it impossible for us to influence the public in any other way but terrorism.

Tarrant donated money to the Identitarian Movement in Austria precisely to "link" it to terrorism and give the state a pretext for suppressing it. That makes him no different from antifa in my eyes. We obviously have no obligations to enemy infiltrators in our movement. Outing them would not be doxing. It would not be betraying comrades. The same would be true of another Tarrant or Bowers. They are not us, and I would rather disavow them to the police before a terrorist incident than disavow them to the press after one.

Moreover, if you state publicly that you will call the police on people threatening terrorism, that makes it far less likely that anyone will talk about such matters in your company, which gives you some security from both sincere cranks and enemy provocateurs.

Terrorism is a desperate measure. And desperate times call for desperate measures. But I want to argue that times aren't quite so desperate as some people think. Yes, as I argue in my book *The White Nationalist Manifesto* that long-term demographic trends for white people are alarming. If we do not halt existing demographic trends, we're first going to lose control of all of our homelands, and then we're simply going to become extinct as a race.

But the worst-case scenario of extinction still lies a couple of centuries off. And even in parts of the white world where the majority of births are now of non-whites, it will still be some decades before these people have voting rights and can exercise political power. And by the time that happens, you might find that a lot of whites will be willing to limit the franchise or do away with voting altogether.

So we have some decades to fix things: twenty years, thirty years, fifty years, depending on what country we're in. This means that we have plenty of time to think very carefully about the right way to regain control over our homelands. Things are not so desperate that people should be contemplating acts of violence.

Furthermore, while it is true that the long-term demographic trends are alarming, there are a lot of medium-term social and political trends that are working in our favor. I wish to recommend the book *National Populism* by two British political scientists, Roger Eatwell and Matthew Goodwin.[1] They argue that four trends are giving rise to national populism.

---

[1] Roger Eatwell and Matthew Goodwin, *National Populism: The Revolt Against Liberal Democracy* (New York: Pelican, 2018).

The first is *distrust*. The people's distrust of the establishment is rising in every white country. I am sure that social distrust is at an all-time high in Great Britain now that it is clear that the establishment does not want to deliver Brexit, the people be damned. Rising distrust in the establishment means that people will increasingly consider radical alternatives like White Nationalism.

The second trend is *destruction*, specifically the destruction of identity by multiculturalism and immigration. Eatwell and Goodwin actually argue that there's nothing morally objectionable about a people wishing to maintain the ethnic and cultural constitution of its homeland. There is nothing wrong with wanting to pass a country on to your children that resembles the one in which you were born. Thus people are increasingly voting for national populist measures that will halt multiculturalism and immigration.

The third trend is *deprivation*, specifically the destruction of working-class and middle-class living standards by globalization. That is also driving people toward populism because populists promise protectionism and re-industrialization, which is a powerful message to people who increasingly feel that their children and grandchildren are facing harder, poorer lives.

The final trend is *de-alignment*, which simply means that as more people want national populist policies, they will abandon their ties to the established center-Left and center-Right political parties.

Eatwell and Goodwin argue that all four of these trends are deep-seated and will not abate any time soon. In fact, they believe that the only way to stem the populist tide is for the political establishment to adopt populist measures. Which means that the hegemony of globalism is ending, and national populism is taking its place. White Nationalism is merely the most radical and consistent form of national populism. And as more people become receptive to our message, we will have opportunities to move politics in our direction for decades to come. So now is not the time to give in to people in the grip of self-marginalizing and self-defeating behaviors.

But even if you believe that time is too short for intelligent action, doing something stupid and self-defeating won't save us anyway. So you should still do the right thing—and hope that you were wrong about the time frame, so things will all work out.

Now I want to deal briefly with some of the moral arguments that people have made in defense of Tarrant and other White Nationalist terrorists.

Don't people have a right to self-defense, individually and collectively? Yes, of course we do. If someone attacks you, you should respond appropriately.

But terrorist acts don't look like self-defense. They look like aggression against innocent people. Now maybe you disagree with that. Maybe you think that people should see such acts as self-defense. So we are back to the problem of changing the public mind.

There is a difference between an act and its meaning. In terms of producing actual political change, the meaning is more important than the act itself. And right now, our enemies are in the position to tell our people what terrorist acts mean. Which entails that the only concrete political changes that we can expect from White Nationalist terrorism are further censorship and deplatforming directed at racially conscious white people.

Someone actually asked me, "What's the difference between Brenton Tarrant and Charles Martel?" And the answer is very simple. Charles Martel was a legitimate leader who had his people behind him, whereas Tarrant was a lone gunman who is now execrated as a moral freak and monster. There are fewer people who sympathize with our views after his attack than before it. If you don't like that situation, what are you going to do about it? Obviously, you are going to have to change the public mind.

Others argue that if our government is corrupt and in cahoots with criminals and invaders, we have a right to take up arms. Isn't there a right to be a vigilante against injustice? Isn't there a right to revolution? And I would say yes, absolutely. A government that does not govern in the interest of its people is illegitimate, and we don't just have a *right* to overthrow it, we've got an *obligation* to do so.

The only question is: How do we go about this? What's the most rational way to change the regime? And again, before you begin, you have to look at your strengths and weaknesses, and those of your enemy, and then work out a course of action. And Tarrant chose poorly. His plan was to promote a crackdown on free expression and gun rights. This, he thought, would make people so angry that—even in the absence of weapons or the ability to communicate with one another—they would *somehow* come together to launch a popular revolution. Yes, his plan was that dumb.

So yes, people have a right to self-defense. Yes, people have the right to take justice into their own hands when the state fails them. Yes, people have the right to overthrow unjust regimes. But the difference between success and failure in each of these ventures depends in large part on whether public opinion is on your side or not. Thus, in each case, we must begin by changing people's minds. In each case, we must first worry about securing the metapolitical conditions of political success.

Some people have outrageously misrepresented this as "doing nothing." Of course their objections consist merely of words on the internet. So if I am "doing nothing" then so are my critics. In fact, however, we are all doing something very important. We are arguing about what makes victory possible. In short, we are doing metapolitics.

Sun Tzu once said, "Victorious warriors win first and then go to war, while defeated warriors go to war first and then seek to win." To "win first" means to prepare the necessary conditions of victory before one goes into battle. That is analogous to metapolitics. Terrorists like Tarrant, however, first go into battle and then hope that somehow, somebody else will fashion a victory for them. Such folly is the road to defeat.

I can't help but think that such strategic stupidity is fed, in part, by the Alt Right's pervasive ethos of ironism and frivolity. If so, then it is time to smack the Alt-Right smirk off the movement's face. We will never be equal to the most serious crisis our race has ever faced until we are much more serious men.

Counter-Currents, April 28, 2019

AGAINST ACCELERATIONISM

Accelerationism is the idea that the best way to achieve White Nationalist goals is to accelerate the decline of the present system. This will supposedly have two effects. First, acceleration will weaken the system's ability to maintain power, including to oppress dissenters. Second, acceleration will anger and awaken the white masses, making them more receptive to our message.

Accelerationism is often associated with the maxim, "Worse is better." As a categorical statement, "Worse is better" is just a contradiction in terms, like "Bad is good," "Night is day," and "Losing is winning." But there is a qualified sense in which that maxim is true: What is worse for the present system is generally better for dissidents.[1] We all know that the system is going in the wrong direction: demographically, culturally economically, and politically. The sooner these problems manifest themselves, the sooner dissidents can step forward with alternatives—and the sooner resistance to our plans will crumble.

Furthermore, the present political system offers only two options: the Left, which wants to accelerate "progress" toward complete social breakdown, and the Right, which merely wants to slow the process down and perhaps put it on firmer economic and social foundations. Accelerationists thus conclude that it might be better to have the Left in power, so it destabilizes and hastens the end of the system.

Then they talk about the frog. No, not Pepe. No, not

---

[1] Greg Johnson, "'Worse Is Better,'" *New Right vs. Old Right* (San Francisco: Counter-Currents, 2013).

the one with the scorpion. No, not the singing frog from the Warner Bros. cartoon. The frog in the pan of water. If you want to boil a frog, you have to do it slowly, so he doesn't realize what is happening and jump out of the pan. By slowing down "progress," the mainstream Right lulls the frog into a false sense of security. But the Left, by accelerating the process, might cause the frog to get antsy and jump out of the pan.

But not everything that is bad for the establishment is good for dissidents. Wars, economic crashes, and natural disasters can affect dissidents as well as the ruling elite. Declining trust in the government and media obviously helps dissidents. But an across-the-board decline in social trust would probably strengthen whoever holds power. When black rule came to South Africa and Rhodesia, the ongoing disasters did not galvanize white self-assertion.

Worse (for them) is not necessarily better (for us). Worse is sometimes just worse. So praying for bad news—or actively promoting bad outcomes—seems like a very foolish way to create a better world. In fact, it seems akin to suicide bombing: an act of a people reduced to hopelessness and desperation after a long train of defeats.

So where does accelerationism come from? It begins as a psychological mechanism for coping with defeat. For instance, imagine you convinced yourself that it was vitally important for white Americans that Mitt Romney defeat Barack Obama in 2012. When Romney lost, you might have consoled yourself with the thought that maybe four more years of Obama wouldn't be so bad after all, since he might accelerate the system's decline and redpill more normies. It isn't an unreasonable position.

But there's an important distinction here. There is a world of difference between (1) doing what one thinks is right, suffering defeat, and then hoping, in retrospect, that the bad consequences you tried to fight might hasten the eventual triumph of the true and the good—and (2) taking accelerationism as a first principle and actively promoting bad ideas and policies because you think they will hasten the triumph of the true and the good.

For instance, accelerationism was the basis of Brenton Tarrant's scheme to use terrorism to provoke state repression of freedom of speech, gun rights, and open white advocates—on the assumption that this would somehow spark a White Nationalist revolution—a revolution that would somehow be organized without the ability to communicate and somehow triumph without access to weapons. But we do not win by losing our freedom of speech, our right to bear arms, or our right to organize and participate in political life. That's how we lose.

In 2008 and 2012, I argued that the election of Barack Obama would be better for White Nationalism than the election of John McCain and Mitt Romney.[2] After all, McCain and Romney would have done nothing to halt non-white immigration and white demographic decline. Instead, they would have simply put white faces on an anti-white system and lulled the Right into complacency. They might have also put the system on sounder economic and political footing.

Obama, by contrast, put a non-white face on an anti-white system. He made white dispossession visible. Being a Leftist, he was also more likely to push too far, too fast and destabilize the system. I thought that McCain and Romney offered nothing to White Nationalists but that Obama would give us opportunities for progress. So I did not oppose him.

---

[2] Greg Johnson, "The 2008 Presidential Election" and "The 2012 US Presidential Election," *Confessions of a Reluctant Hater*.

You can call that accelerationism if you like. But, by the same token, I did not *vote* for Obama, because there's a difference between *hoping* that good will come out of evil and *knowing* it. I believe it is our duty to do good and fight evil. If the gods want to turn evil into good, that lies in their power, not ours. Moreover, I knew my individual vote would not have mattered anyway, so I would have felt foolish wasting my time voting. Beyond that, I would have still felt vaguely dirty casting even a meaningless vote for Obama.

Furthermore, if Obama ran on the platforms being promoted by today's Democrats—namely censoring White Nationalists, grabbing guns, and abolishing the borders—and McCain or Romney opposed those policies, I would have supported them enthusiastically.

In 2016, I had a very different attitude toward the Republican nominee, because Donald Trump had broken with Republican orthodoxy on immigration, free trade, and foreign policy. He was defending immigration restriction, protectionism, and an America First foreign policy. These were *our* issues. It was a huge win for us when Trump simply created a *debate* about these ideas, because none of the other candidates would have done so, and because we can *win* such debates.

Also note that this was a win for us no matter what happened next: whether Trump won or lost the election, whether Trump succeeded or failed in implementing his policies. But of course, we wanted Trump to win the election and then triumph over the congress, the press, and the deep state to implement his policies, because it would have been "our" victory. Not a complete victory, of course. But it would have been a significant step in the right direction.

Thus I was very impatient with accelerationist talk in 2016. I actually heard people say that maybe we should support Hillary Clinton, you know, to *accelerate* things.

At this point, it became clear to me that accelerationism had mutated from a coping mechanism into a toxic "strategy" that basically amounts to the claim that "We win by losing."

It would have been perfectly understandable to advance such ideas if Trump had actually lost. But when our ideas were actually threatening to win out, it was the height of perversity to suggest that we snatch defeat from the jaws of victory because we somehow win by losing.

No, actually we lose by losing. When we lose, we can of course hope that somehow the gods or "history" will turn our defeats into conditions for future victories. But in the end, we can only win by winning.

Counter-Currents, July 22, 2019

Epstein's Death & the Conspiracy Canard

When Jeffrey Epstein died on August 10, 2019, he was one of the world's most important prisoners because of the people he might implicate in his crimes.

Epstein was charged with multiple counts of sex trafficking and conspiracy to traffic minors for sex. But he was no ordinary pervert or pimp. Epstein enjoyed enormous wealth from obscure origins. He was described as a financier but had only one known client, Les Wexner, owner of Victoria's Secret and other companies.

Epstein used his wealth to buy his way into the upper echelons of the American-Anglo-Jewish political and financial elite. Epstein's black book contained contact information for such people as Donald Trump, Bill Clinton, Queen Elizabeth II, Prince Andrew, King Salman of Saudi Arabia, Alan Dershowitz, Ehud Barak, Henry Kissinger, Michael Bloomberg, and many other oligarchs and entertainers.

Epstein apparently had a taste for underage girls. Underage girls, of course, cannot legally consent to sex, so Jeffrey Epstein was a serial rapist. He widely advertised his tastes, calling his private jet the *Lolita Express*. In 2006, the FBI began investigating Epstein, tracking down more than 100 women, many of them underage, who had been paid to perform sex acts for Epstein and his wealthy and influential friends.

But in 2007, Epstein cut a deal with US Attorney Alex Acosta to avoid federal prosecution and prison. According to the terms of this agreement, Epstein agreed to plead guilty to two felony prostitution charges in state court. In exchange, Epstein and his accomplices received immunity from federal sex-trafficking charges that could have land-ed them in prison for life. Epstein served thirteen months in a private wing in a county jail. He was allowed to leave the jail sixteen hours a day, six days a week. Basically, he only slept there. His alleged accomplices were never prosecuted. The Epstein deal was sealed, so that the nature and full extent of his crimes were never made public. The Epstein case was unsealed earlier this year due to the efforts of reporter Julie Brown, leading to Epstein's arrest and eventually to his death.[1]

Acosta ended up as Secretary of Labor in the Trump Administration. Acosta reportedly told a White House official, who then told reporter Vicky Ward, that he had signed the non-prosecution agreement because he had been told to "back off" on Epstein. "I was told Epstein 'belonged to intelligence' and to leave it alone."[2] If this is true, one has to ask: Which country's intelligence services did Epstein belong to? And who told Acosta to back off?

Philip Giraldi suggests Israel as a likely candidate.[3] Epstein was Jewish. So is his one known client, Les Wexner. His former girlfriend, confidante, and alleged co-conspirator in sex trafficking is Ghislaine Maxwell, the daughter of Robert Maxwell (born Ján Ludvík Hyman Binyamin Hoch), a wealthy Jewish businessman and swindler who, like Epstein, died under mysterious circumstances. According to Giraldi, "After his death, [Maxwell] was given a state funeral by Israel in which six serving and former heads of Israeli intelligence listened while Prime Minister Yitzhak Shamir eulogized: 'He has done more for Israel than can today be said.'"

---

[1] Julie K. Brown, "How a Future Trump Cabinet Member Gave a Serial Sex Abuser the Deal of a Lifetime," *Miami Herald*, November 28, 2018.

[2] Vicky Ward, "Jeffrey Epstein's Sick Story Played Out for Years in Plain Sight," *Daily Beast*, July 9, 2019.

[3] Philip Giraldi, "Did Pedophile Jeffrey Epstein Work for Mossad?," *The Unz Review*, July 11, 2019.

All of this raises uncomfortable questions. Was Epstein entrapping his wealthy and influential friends into committing statutory rape? Was he also collecting other more or less embarrassing dirt on them, in order to financially and perhaps politically blackmail them?[4] That's my working hypothesis.

I think Jeffrey Epstein was probably an Israeli intelligence agent, given the cover of a wealthy and connected financier, who pimped out underage girls to wealthy and influential perverts so he could blackmail them for money and favors in business and politics. This theory fits the known facts, has predictive power, and can be verified or refuted by further investigation. If this hypothesis is true, then quite a few powerful people had reasons to ensure that Epstein never stood trial or cut a deal with the prosecution.

Now if I knew Epstein was a likely target for assassination, so did the people who prosecuted him. So did Epstein's jailers at New York's Metropolitan Correctional Center. *Everybody* should have known that Epstein was a target as soon as he was arrested on July 6, 2019. Those who somehow initially overlooked this fact certainly had no excuse after Epstein was found injured and semiconscious in his cell on July 23, 2019. Epstein had marks around his neck consistent with either attempted suicide or attempted murder. To make matters worse, Epstein and his cellmate dummied up about what happened.

Thus when Jeffrey Epstein turned up dead with marks around his neck consistent with murder or suicide, everyone with two IQ points to rub together and a cursory knowledge of his case concluded that his death was *no mere suicide*.

Let's think this through. *Jeffrey Epstein was either mur-*

---

[4] Matt Stieb, "How Jeffrey Epstein Made His Money: Four Wild Theories," *New York Magazine*, July 9, 2019.

dered or he committed suicide. Nobody has suggested that Epstein died of natural causes. I am surprised nobody has suggested auto-erotic asphyxiation, given what a colossal pervert he was.

Because the Metropolitan Correctional Center had ways to prevent Epstein from committing suicide, if it was suicide, then Epstein was *allowed* to kill himself. If he was allowed to kill himself, it was either *intentional* or *negligent*.

If Epstein was intentionally allowed to kill himself, then the probable motive is the same as murder, namely to prevent Epstein from testifying.

If Epstein was negligently allowed to kill himself, then we have to conclude that the US government, particularly in New York City, is no longer a serious institution. Instead, it is functioning on a level somewhere between a Latin American banana republic and an African failed state. In particular, we have to conclude that the people in charge of New York's Metropolitan Correctional Center are either criminal or negligent, or perhaps a combination of the two.

Moreover, any intelligent person could have concluded all of this *before* we began hearing stories of mysteriously malfunctioning surveillance cameras, mysteriously discontinued suicide monitoring, and mysteriously absent guards.

Whether it is murder or suicide, Jeffrey Epstein's death is the scandal of the decade. Whether it is murder or suicide, and whether we ever get the truth or not, the Epstein case can only further unravel the average American's already frayed trust in the political system and mainstream media. And that's really good for populist dissidents like me, for populism feeds on the breakdown of trust in the establishment.

When the Epstein debate is between those who think that the system was *evil enough to murder him* or *incompe-*

tent enough to let him commit suicide, the system can't win, and we dissidents can't lose. No matter what happened, the truth hurts them and helps us.

But what if we never even learn the truth? Then the debate will be between people who think the system is *evil enough to cover up the truth* and the people who think the system is *too incompetent to find it*. Heads we dissidents win, tails the establishment loses.

I like those odds.

Furthermore, something else died on August 10th, 2019, something of potentially far greater import than Jeffrey Epstein: The phrase "conspiracy theory" lost its power to deter critical thinking about the consensus manufactured and imposed by the political and media establishment.

In the hands of the establishment, "conspiracy theory" is simply a term of abuse masquerading as an objective category. For the establishment, a "conspiracy theory" is just a dissenting viewpoint that threatens its power.

But there's nothing wrong with conspiracy theories. A "theory" is simply an explanation that ties together observed phenomena in terms of an underlying set of causes, e.g., the theory of evolution or atomic theory. A "conspiracy theory" is an explanation that ties together observed phenomena in terms of underlying causes as well, in this case *human planning*. The Latin root of "conspiracy," *conspirare*, means to "whisper together."

A conspiracy is a kind of human planning and action that has two essential characteristics. First, a conspiracy requires at least two people. An idea hatched and carried out by a lone person may be a plot or a crime, but it is not a conspiracy. Second, a conspiracy requires secrecy, because the things that people conspire about cannot be discussed openly without endangering the plan.

Conspiracies are often criminal but need not be. Sometimes one must resort to conspiracies to do perfectly legal things because to plan and act openly would tip one's hand to rivals and enemies. So when football players huddle, they are conspiring. When businessmen develop products, they are conspiring. When governments plan espionage and warfare, they are conspiring. When political parties and candidates plan election campaigns, they are conspiring. When dissidents plan meetings and events, they are conspiring. I conspire every day of my life, from dawn to dusk.

Much of human history springs from plans and actions that begin in secret. Thus to stigmatize conspiracy theories as such would require us to throw out a vast number of criminal prosecutions. The same goes for most journalism and historiography, which often seek to tie together multiple observed facts in terms of unified plans. Most of the best literature and film on politics, espionage, and crime would have to be discarded as well. Can you imagine a James Bond movie in which merely uttering the words "conspiracy theory" would paralyze thought and action?

Moreover, the very same people who denigrate "conspiracy theories" engage in them all the time. But they don't present them as theories. They just pass them off as facts. Consider this howler from Julia Ebner, who begins her essay "Stop the Online Conspiracy Theories Before They Break Democracy" with the words: "Organised conspiracy theorist networks have launched an all-out information war across Europe."[5] Of course, an "organized network" is just a clumsy way of saying "conspiracy."

For the Left, Russia collusion, patriarchy, and white privilege are not conspiracy theories. They're just facts. Which means that a "conspiracy theory" is just something that the establishment doesn't want you to believe. A

---

[5] Julia Ebner, "Stop the Online Conspiracy Theories Before They Break Democracy," *The Guardian*, February 18, 2019.

"conspiracy theory" is just a "dissenting idea," which means that Ebner's real title should be "Stop the Online Dissenting Ideas Before They Break Democracy."

I'll bet you thought that one feature of democracy is *protecting* dissenting ideas. That is certainly the purpose of the First Amendment in the United States. Freedom of speech needs to be a constitutional right to allow people to *dissent* from the opinions of the powerful, who might otherwise censor and punish disagreement.[6]

Like "discrimination" and "generalization,"[7] which the establishment also stigmatize as wicked, conspiracy theorizing—like theorizing in general—is simply a form of intelligence. Theorizing is what smart people do when faced with bewildering and complex phenomena. An establishment that praises credulity and stupidity is obviously up to no good.

Indeed, attacking conspiracy theories as such is an act of desperation. If truth is on your side, then it should be easy to refute contrary positions. The only reason one would want to disqualify dissent *as such* is the inability to refute dissenting views on their individual merits. But that's exactly what one would expect from a system founded on lies, particularly the strange, self-contradictory lie that people are all equal and their differences are always a source of strength.

Conspiracy theorizing has been rising in recent years as trust in the establishment declines, and the establishment was pushing back. Before Epstein's death, there was an alarming trend to weaponize the "conspiracy theory" smear to silence dissidents.

For instance, on August 6, 2018, Facebook, Apple's

---

[6] See Greg Johnson, "Freedom of Speech," *Toward a New Nationalism*.

[7] See Greg Johnson, "In Defense of Prejudice," *In Defense of Prejudice* (San Francisco: Counter-Currents, 2017).

iTunes, YouTube, and Spotify removed all content by conspiracy theorist Alex Jones and his *InfoWars* site from their platforms. What's the most plausible explanation for all four platforms dumping Jones on the same day: conspiracy or coincidence?

In January of 2019, YouTube announced that it would tweak its algorithms to recommend fewer "conspiracy theory" videos.[8] Of course, YouTube does not define Russia collusion as a conspiracy theory, but it does brand white genocide and the Great Replacement as conspiracy theories.

Then on August 1, 2019, *Yahoo! News* reported on an FBI intelligence bulletin from the bureau's Phoenix field office, dated May 30, 2019, which identified "conspiracy theories" like Pizzagate and QAnon to be domestic terrorist threats.[9]

But since Epstein's death, "conspiracy theories" are no longer marginal. They are mainstream.

Donald Trump has retweeted speculations that Bill Clinton was behind Epstein's death. Democrats, for their part, are floating the theory that Trump was behind Epstein's demise. Both Trump and Clinton are womanizers who knew Epstein.

Former New York Mayor and prosecutor Rudolph Giuliani pronounced the story of Epstein's suicide "incredible" and claimed that there are "probably 50 very important people that have a motive to kill him."[10]

---

[8] Julia Carrie Wong and Sam Levin, "YouTube Vows to Recommend Fewer Conspiracy Theory Videos," *The Guardian*, January 25, 2019.

[9] Jana Winter, "FBI Document Warns Conspiracy Theories Are a New Domestic Terrorism Threat," *Yahoo! News*, August 1, 2019.

[10] Daniel Chaitin, "Giuliani: Probably 50 'very important people' Wanted Jeffrey Epstein Dead," *The Washington Examiner*, August 13, 2019.

Current New York Mayor Bill De Blasio agreed, saying that Epstein's death was "way too convenient" and could not be attributed to "traditional human error."[11] De Blasio basically said, "I'm not a conspiracy theorist, but . . ." Or, as De Blasio put it, "sometimes you see a series of events that you cannot give a normal explanation for, and there needs to be a full investigation"—which pretty much sums up the feelings of conspiracy theorists on this matter.

Since Epstein's death, media attempts to contain speculation with the "conspiracy theory" canard have been rather half-hearted, with the lamest attempts coming from the most authoritative sources. For instance, the BBC clucks disapprovingly that "[j]ust hours after the high-profile financier Jeffrey Epstein was found dead on Saturday, unsubstantiated theories about his death began to gain traction online."[12]

Epstein's death is *obviously* fishy to any intelligent person. So *of course* people immediately began to speculate about alternative scenarios. Complaining that such theories are "unsubstantiated" is silly. Of course they are unsubstantiated. There had not been enough time to substantiate them. Every theory is unsubstantiated before it is tested. That's why we need to test them. Let's put some of the BBC's investigative journalists to work on that, shall we? But apparently people at the BBC would like you to suspend judgment about the Epstein case and simply believe what they tell you.

After Epstein, we're all conspiracy theorists now. The distinction between marginal "conspiracy theories" and mainstream "facts" has collapsed. The only relevant dis-

---

[11] Mike Brest, "'Way too convenient': De Blasio Speculates About Epstein's Death, *The Washington Examiner*, August 14, 2019.

[12] "Jeffrey Epstein: How Conspiracy Theories Spread After Financier's Death," *BBC News*, August 12, 2019.

tinction now is between *good* conspiracy theories and *bad* ones, *true* conspiracies and *false* ones.

Conspiracy theories are organically connected with populism. Populism holds that government is legitimate only if it governs for the common good. Populists regard factions and special interests as inimical to good government. Populists believe that government deliberations should be maximally transparent to guard against subversion by special interests, which must conspire in secret against the public good.

As I argued above, Epstein's death helps populists no matter the outcome of the case. First and foremost, Epstein's death has deprived "conspiracy theory" of its power to marginalize, stigmatize, and paralyze critical thinking. Second, no matter what side of the Epstein debate you take, the system loses: If Epstein was murdered or intentionally allowed to commit suicide, the system is *evil*. If Epstein was negligently allowed to commit suicide, then the system is *incompetent*. If we never learn the truth about Epstein's death, then the debate will be between those who think the system is *evil enough to cover up the truth* or *too incompetent to discover it*.

Please note that none of these populist gains are contingent on ever discovering the truth about Epstein's death. The system has already written off these losses and moved on, leaving us to capitalize on them. The *best-case scenario* for the system entails a catastrophic loss of public trust, prestige, and narrative control.

It's almost as if Epstein's death was engineered by people who have no investment in the long-term viability of the American system. Perhaps America isn't their country. Or maybe they simply fear a much worse outcome.

Which makes me wonder: What would happen if the system's worst-case scenario came true, namely that we learn the full truth about Jeffrey Epstein and his friends? Given the waning power of the conspiracy canard and the role of genuine investigative journalism in bringing Epstein's crimes to light, there is some reason for hope. But we shouldn't wait around for such an eventuality. Instead, we should be capitalizing on the gains the Epstein case has already handed us.

Counter-Currents, August 19, 2019

THE PARANOID STYLE IN WHITE NATIONALISM

If you think this essay is about you, you might be paranoid.

Guardians of the conventional wisdom frequently accuse White Nationalists of being "paranoid" when we express fears of non-white crime, white demographic decline, race replacement immigration, and ultimately white extinction and white genocide.

White Nationalists are also frequently accused of "phobias" like "xenophobia" (the fear of aliens).

These accusations are not psychiatric diagnoses. They are not offered to help us. They are just cheap rhetorical attacks, attempts to dismiss our concerns as irrational. By pathologizing our views, our enemies seek to frighten off conventional-minded people who might otherwise take our ideas seriously. They might even gaslight the weakest among us into doubting their own sanity.

But in truth, White Nationalist fears of non-white crime, multiculturalism, and race-replacement immigration are quite reasonable. Even our most alarming ideas—white extinction and white genocide—are, unfortunately, based on objective facts and sober analysis.[1]

Jewish historian Richard Hofstadter's 1964 essay "The Paranoid Style in American Politics"[2] is often name-dropped as a classic treatment of political paranoia, but it is a disappointingly superficial magazine article, published in *Harpers* in November of 1964 against the backdrop of

---

[1] See Greg Johnson, "White Extinction" and "White Genocide," *The White Nationalist Manifesto*.

[2] Richard Hofstadter, "The Paranoid Style in American Politics," *Harpers*, November 1964.

the Barry Goldwater–Lyndon Johnson presidential race.

Hofstadter does not *reflect* on the idea of paranoia; he simply *uses* it in an attempt to pathologize conspiracy theories and gaslight people who are inclined to think in conspiratorial terms. Nor does Hofstadter refute any of the conspiracy theories he mocks, and for good reason: They all have more than a kernel of truth, particularly Senator Joseph McCarthy's warnings of communist infiltration of the US government.

Frankly, the only good feature of Hofstadter's essay is its title, which is why it is more often cited than read. I'm going to steal the phrase "the paranoid style" because, although the *central claims* of White Nationalism cannot be dismissed as paranoid, *some* people in our movement really do have a paranoid *style*—if not out-and-out paranoia—so the phenomenon needs to be taken seriously.

What follows are some notes on the paranoid style that will help us to identify it, with the ultimate aim of ridding ourselves of it.

First of all, the paranoid style is bad optics. We are constantly being accused of paranoia and various phobias. There are easy *arguments* to counter these claims, but the best refutation is a matter of *action*. We simply should not behave like people in the grip of irrational fears.

Second, the paranoid style is never far removed from actual paranoia, and crazy people don't belong in a serious movement.

"Paranoia" literally means being out of one's mind, from the Greek roots "para," meaning outside or beside, and "noos," meaning the mind. But paranoia refers to a much more specific form of derangement, namely *holding irrational beliefs*—but not just any irrational beliefs: *irrational beliefs motivated by fear*. Paranoids have irrational fears. The *things* they fear are irrational, and the *way* they fear them is irrational.

Fear is not necessarily irrational. Bad things happen all

the time. By its nature, rational action pursues the good and avoids the bad. Whenever one is about to act, it is entirely reasonable to ask, "What's the worst that could happen?" among all other possible outcomes.

Paranoids don't just fear the worst, they *believe* the worst, and they do so *compulsively* and *irrationally*. What makes a fear irrational? It is irrational to fear things that are *unreal* or *unlikely to happen*. Paranoids, however, can't help it. For paranoids, *fearing is believing*.

In my experience, paranoids are not just delusional. They also want you to *share* their delusions, for if you share their delusions, the delusions seem more real, and the paranoids feel less alone. Paranoia is a lonely and terrifying place. Paranoid ideation is not pleasant. It is a self-destructive compulsion akin to drug addiction. Paranoids are like moths frantically fluttering around a lightbulb until they die in fits of agony.

But how does one convince people of delusions? To do this, paranoids generally resort to two techniques: demanding that you treat them as authorities, so you simply accept their core delusions on faith, and making up tissues of lies that support belief in the core delusion. This is akin to the "pious fraud" who makes up stories about divine revelations and miracles to support core religious articles of faith.

One wonders if paranoids *consciously* lie to shore up their delusions or if some of them really believe the stories they improvise on the spot. Surely some of them are conscious liars who take pleasure in duping others because it makes them feel powerful. Naturally, if paranoids are willing simply to lie, they are also willing to use all lesser forms of deceptive rhetoric and emotional manipulation as well, and when those fail, some will move to screaming rage and physical assault.

The worst-case scenario in a debate is that one's opponent is intellectually dishonest. Thus in debates, paranoids tend to go straight to accusations of bad faith. For paranoids, there are no honest disagreements or honorable opponents. There are simply bad actors and venal shills. Since most of our movement consists of exchanging ideas online, such accusations are generally the first sign that one is dealing with a paranoid.

Of course there really are intellectually dishonest people, but the problem with paranoids is their lack of evidence and their rush to judgment. Paranoids are often lightning-fast because they move from suspicion to certainty without the necessity of gathering and weighing evidence. The best way to counter them is to slow them down and ask for evidence. "Now wait just a minute there, sonny..."

Since paranoids come off as cranks, they usually have plenty of opponents, a number that only increases with time. If one has many intellectual opponents, the worst-case scenario is that they are all conspiring together behind the scenes. Thus paranoids routinely describe their opponents as parts of sinister "conspiracies," "alliances," "axes," "cults," "mafias," and other networks, imagining all sorts of covert horse-trading, handshakes, and maneuvers to swindle the paranoid out of his just deserts.

Of course such conspiracies can actually exist, but the problem with paranoids is their hasty reasoning and lack of evidence. Paranoids like to paint ballroom-sized canvases with broad brushes at furious speed. So the best way to respond is to focus in on the details and ask if they are based on fact and if they are really connected with one another. "Cool story. But is it true?"

In my experience, paranoia is also often connected with narcissism. I have already discussed one aspect of the paranoid's narcissism: his desire to convince an audience of his delusions. But narcissism is not just a fruit of paranoia, it is also a root of it, especially narcissistic delusions of grandeur. If one has an inflated self-image, the fact that other people seldom share it requires an explanation. Since a narcissist by his very nature is resistant to revising his self-image, he has to conclude that something is wrong with other people. They would acknowledge his superiority, if only they were not stupid or jealous or malevolent.

Furthermore, since it is inconceivable to a narcissist that many different people would independently draw the same negative conclusions about him, he is again drawn to conspiratorial explanations, positing the existence of whispering campaigns whereby a few malevolent people spread lies around like a cold virus.

Again, envy and coordinated campaigns of slander are real human phenomena, so one can't dismiss such explanations out of hand. Instead, one has to ask for evidence.

Another trait I have noticed in paranoids is a tendency toward categorical, binary, and all-or-nothing thinking. Categorical statements are absolute and unqualified. In a binary situation, there are only two options. One binary option is all-or-nothing.

Of course, there really are categorical truths. There really are binary situations, including all-or-nothing options. But one needs to offer *evidence* for them. The paranoid mind is drawn toward such thinking, regardless of evidence, because of an irrational attraction to the extreme and momentous, especially if accompanied by a frisson of fear.

There's also an element of intellectual laziness to such claims.

A paranoid might wish to argue that something about Trump's foreign policy is not as it seems, but instead of offering specific evidence, he simply announces a categorical metaphysical statement: "Nothing is what it seems."

A paranoid might want to argue that a certain event was not a coincidence, but instead of offering specific evidence for his thesis, he simply resorts to the categorial metaphysical statement: "There are no accidents."

A paranoid might wish to establish that two apparently unconnected events are actually covertly connected, but instead of actually showing the connection, he appeals to a categorical metaphysical statement: "Everything is connected."

Another feature of the paranoid style is to put the stamp of eternity on things, because a problem that has *always* existed is worse than a problem that emerges at a specific time under specific conditions. For instance, Donald Trump is not a disappointment because he failed to implement his most important promises—immigration restriction and America First in trade and foreign policy—in the face of stiff opposition. No, Trump is a *fraud*, because that is the worst-case scenario. But there's something still worse than being a fraud, hence the accusation that Trump was *always* a fraud. He *never meant* to keep those promises.

Yes, some things are forever, but most aren't, thus here too it comes down to a question of evidence.

There's also an element of narcissistic preening to claiming that one has *always* had the *inside* scoop.

But aren't paranoids sometimes right? Yes, but that should not give them any credibility. If you believe the worst about everybody, sometimes you will be right, but *merely by accident*, in the same way that a stopped clock is right twice a day. But if you happen to glance at a stopped clock at the right time of day, that is no reason to regard the instrument as reliable. In the same way, the paranoid mind is not a reliable guide to the truth, even though sometimes it might stumble on the truth by accident.

Not everyone who exhibits the paranoid style is actually paranoid. But there are enough paranoids in the White Nationalist milieu that others have picked up their tropes by osmosis. This is a problem, because, at core, White Nationalism is an intellectual movement. We are a vast online educational project.

But, unfortunately, we are also a school for unreason because this movement has no barriers to the entry of crazy people, nor any ways to quarantine or expel them. The best we can do is inoculate ourselves against such influences by teaching our people how to spot and avoid them.

This is crucially important, because at present, our movement's greatest strengths are truth, intellectual rigor, and the credibility they grant us in a culture based on lies and unreason. We need to guard these advantages zealously from both critics without and crazies within.

Counter-Currents, January 13, 2020

Principles are More Important Than People

There is a lot of wisdom in the anonymous saying: "Great minds discuss ideas. Average minds discuss events. Small minds discuss people."

But understanding this saying requires some nuances. One can't understand politics without discussing *all three* categories: ideas, events, and people.

Thus great minds do not discuss *only* ideas. They also discuss events and people. But they understand them in the light of ideas.

Average minds don't simply discuss events. They also discuss people. But ideas are above them, which is what makes them average.

Small minds simply discuss people, because ideas and events are somehow beyond them, which is what makes them small minded.

It is easy to discuss people, so everybody does it. It is harder to discuss events, so only average and above-average people do it. It is even harder to discuss ideas, so only above-average people do it.

Small minds tend to think that everything is a matter of personality. Average and above-average minds understand that personality is important, but personality is not all there is to politics. Average minds recognize that events can't be reduced to just personalities. Events can take on a life of their own. But only the broadest minds recognize that one also needs to talk about principles as well as events and personalities.

I also think speaking of "great" minds raises the bar too high, for it makes one think of Aristotle or Goethe. But one doesn't need to be a genius to recognize the important of ideas. Thus I prefer to speak of *broad*, *average*, and *narrow* or *small* minds.

Intelligence is clearly a factor here, but breadth and narrowness are more important, and it is possible for small-minded people to be quite intelligent, within their limited horizons.

In politics, events can be understood as the result of ideas and people interacting. Both ideas and personalities leave their mark on history. But what is more important for understanding political events: ideas or personalities?

Two hallmarks of average and small minds are the narrowness of their focus and the shortness of their time horizons. If you focus on small-scale events and short time spans, personalities loom larger than ideas in the scheme of things.

But if you step back and focus on larger political trends—trends that can outlast individuals, parties, and nations—then fundamental ideas are decisive. But abstract principles and long time-spans only disclose themselves to broad-minded individuals. They are beyond the ken of the average and small-minded, who bump up against the ceiling of their understanding.

Typical politics is a bitter struggle between the personalities, interest groups, and parties of the Right and the Left. Sometimes the Right is dominant. Sometimes the Left is. Yet if one takes a broader view, one sees that politics drifts steadily to the Left, no matter how bitterly the Right resists. Robert Lewis Dabney brilliantly described this tendency in 1897, when he predicted the success of women's suffrage based on the character of its opponents, the conservatives of his day:

> This is a party which never conserves anything. Its history has been that it demurs to each aggression of the progressive party, and aims to save its credit by a respectable amount of growling, but always acquiesces at last in the innovation. What was the re-

sisted novelty of yesterday is today one of the accepted principles of conservatism; it is now conservative only in affecting to resist the next innovation, which will tomorrow be forced upon its timidity and will be succeeded by some third revolution; to be denounced and then adopted in its turn. American conservatism is merely the shadow that follows Radicalism as it moves forward towards perdition. It remains behind it, but never retards it, and always advances near its leader.[1]

This is because the mainstream Right shares the same basic egalitarian and universalist principles as the Left. But Rightists are just slower to embrace the ultimate consequences of these principles, because the Right is also the party of the bourgeoise, who regard a long and comfortable life as the highest good. Bourgeois conservatives have "got theirs" and are thus morally complacent and fearful of the radical changes required by the next phase of equality's triumphant march through the world.

But the same bourgeois value system that leads to moral complacency also leads to cowardice and compromise. So, over time, the superior moral commitment of the Left, combined with the Right's own latent Leftist premises, ensure continued Leftward drift. Because the Right shares the Left's principles, the Left has a systematic long-term advantage over the Right. Every Rightist's moral convictions are a Leftist fifth column, occupying the highest seats of his government, ending every siege with surrender.

This means that if national populists want to make long-term political gains, we need to focus more on fundamental ideas and not get distracted by ephemeral

---

[1] Robert Lewis Dabney, "Women's Rights Women," *The Southern Magazine*, 1871.

events and personalities.

These are some of the ideological dogmas shared by both the mainstream Left and Right that we need to destroy to secure national populist policies.

Political Universalism: We reject the idea that every human being can be part of a single political community. Political universalism is the root of multiculturalism and multiracialism as well as cultural assimilationist, miscegenationist, and civic nationalist ideas. We reject multiculturalism and multiracialism because they lead to alienation and conflict. We reject cultural assimilationism, miscegenation, and civic nationalism because, although they acknowledge the problems of diversity within the same system, they either try to destroy racial and cultural diversity to make the system work, or they try to paper diversity over with manufactured creedal nationalist pieties. We want to preserve the full diversity of races and cultures by giving them their own homelands. We think immigration and "naturalization" should be restricted to small numbers of people who are genetically and culturally similar to their destination societies.

The Taboo Against "Racism": We reject the idea that racial and ethnic identity, solidarity, pride, and preferences are immoral for white people (and only white people). White identity politics is inevitable, necessary, and moral.

Liberalism: We think that individual liberty, private enterprise, and social equality are genuine values. But whenever they conflict with the common good of society, the common good should have priority. Thus we reject liberalism, defined as the ideology that denies that there is a common good, or denies that the common good can be known, or denies that the common good can be pursued by state action. We stand for the classical philosophical principle that there is a common good of society that can be known and pursued by state action.

THE HYPOCRISY QUESTION

If principles are more important than people, then what should one do if one catches one's enemies betraying their principles? For instance, what should one do if one discovers that a leading advocate of diversity lives in an overwhelmingly homogeneous community? (It is true of practically all of them.)

The small-minded, high time preference type will call his enemy out for hypocrisy, for failing to practice what he preaches. This might impeach the credibility of an ephemeral political actor in the minds of ephemeral political observers—until everyone is distracted by new events. The trouble is that it leaves the presumably evil principle of diversity intact and unscathed. Indeed, if anything this approach strengthens the betrayed principle by demanding that people live by it rather than just pay lip service to it. But for small minds, people loom large, and principles are basically above them, although they are willing to use them as a weapon to "own" particular individuals.

The better approach is to point out the contradiction but then attack the principle that is being betrayed, not the person who betrays it. After all, diversity is not a good thing. It leads to alienation, conflict, social breakdown, and violence. Thus we *want* people to betray diversity. One should congratulate one's opponent for having the good sense not to impose diversity upon himself and his loved ones. But then we should ask him to join us to help bring the blessings of homogeneous white communities to Americans from all walks of life, not just the privileged.

Not all hypocrites are alike. If you betray good principles, that makes you a bad person. But does it make you a bad person to betray evil principles? Quite the contrary. It is *good* not to follow bad principles. If liberalism is evil, then the worst liberals have integrity whereas the best liberals are hypocrites. If multiculturalism is evil, then the worst multiculturalists practice what they preach, and the best are hypocrites. *We should applaud the betrayal of evil principles, not demand that people follow them.*

La Rochefoucauld famously said, "Hypocrisy is a tribute that vice pays to virtue," meaning that hypocrisy is superior to unapologetic vice that does not pay lip service to virtue at all. But when the "virtue" in question is actually a vice, then hypocrisy is not merely a tribute to virtue, hypocrisy really is a virtue, and it should be applauded as such, not denounced.

But this approach only makes sense to broad-minded people who regard principles as more important than people. The narrow minded are happy to uphold evil principles merely to "own" their political opponents for the life of a tweet.

THE TRUMP QUESTION

Now let's apply this analysis to the question of how White Nationalists should approach the Trump question. Consider, for instance, Trump's tweets inviting an America-hating Muslim, Somali-born Representative Ilhan Omar, to go back to her home country.

The broad-minded approach is to use this controversy to talk about ideas. Many Trump supporters were delighted by his statement, because they don't think America benefits at all from importing black Muslims who hate this country. America desperately needs a national conversation about this matter. The Left responded predictably, denouncing Trump as being "racist," as if criticizing non-whites about their views and behaviors is the sin of "racism," an obvious attempt to exempt non-whites from criticism and even from punishment for their crimes. This controversy is an excellent opportunity for White Nationalists to inject our ideas into a national debate and to bring people over to our side.

The small-minded approach is to use this controversy to talk about people. For instance, Richard Spencer appeared briefly on CNN. Instead of talking about the issues raised by this debate, he used the occasion to talk about people: namely Trump, unnamed White Nationalists, and himself. According to Spencer, Trump is a hypocrite because he says racist things but won't follow through on them. Other White Nationalists are fooled, but not Spencer. Instead of challenging the idea that Trump's comments were racist, or the idea that racism is bad, Spencer supported the Leftist message that Trump's comments are racist. Thus he reinforced rather than challenged one of the Left's key principles while condemning Trump and congratulating himself.

The basic Spencer code is to denigrate his natural base while preening as big-brained and grandstanding to the Left. It's not just a posture. It's a whole dance. A comic genius described it as glitter bombing. Sadly, it doesn't leave much time to talk about ideas.

A similar dynamic is at work in the charge that White Nationalists are "supporting Trump" or "fooled by Trump" if White Nationalists defend Trump, his statements, and his policies from unjust Leftist and cuckservative attacks. Again, these charges come from small-minded people bumping into the low ceiling of their people-centered understanding. It does not occur to them that nobody need support Trump the man—in part or in toto—to use him as an occasion to defend good ideas and attack bad ones.

And if Trump is only an occasion to enter the battle of ideas, then it does not matter if he means what he says, or whether he will follow through with his proposals. Obviously, we'd like Trump to be a sincere and effective advocate for pro-white policies. But none of that is in our control. Whining and sharing "Blompf" memes won't change anything. We do, however, have the power to defend good ideas and attack bad ones in whatever public forums are open to us, and we should be grateful for the opportunities Trump continues to present us.

We should, of course, criticize Trump for his genuine errors and failings, for that too is an opportunity to talk about ideas.

But we must guard against railing at Trump like spoiled children. This rhetorical style is common in the remnants of the Alt Right. Phase one of their plan is to rally an ultra-radicalized and alienated political sect by pouring scorn on Trump and the various "boomers" and "normies" who support him. We'll never know what phase two is, because none of these people have thought that far ahead.

It may be fun to skewer "Blompf" for his hypocrisies and follies. It is increasingly easy to do. It may earn you kudos in the ever-shrinking online Alt-Right echo-chamber. But if that is our constituency, then our movement has no future.

Those who are playing a long game recognize that the tens of millions of white Americans who voted for Donald Trump are the natural constituency for national populism in America. The most important thing is to uphold the right principles and communicate them to the national populist electorate that Trump has created and is increasingly disappointing and frustrating. When Trump is gone, it is our job to lead them. But we cannot lead them if we do not connect with them. And we cannot connect with them if we go out of our way to alienate them.

As far as White Nationalists were concerned, this was never just about Trump. It was always about advancing our ideas. Trump was always just an occasion for White Nationalists to enter the political debate. He smashed the Republican gentleman's agreement never to talk about whether global trade and non-white immigration are good for America. It was truly magnificent.

Trump asked the right questions, but at best, his answers were half-measures, and half-implemented half-measures are not the solutions Americans need. They are not what his electorate is increasingly clamoring for. But that too is an opportunity for us.

I think some of the spoiled child reactions to Trump's failures and betrayals come from people who somehow convinced themselves that Trump really was going to save America. But that was never realistic. He was one man, advocating confused civic nationalist half-measures against the whole media and political establishment. Trump was never going to save America. That was always our job. It still is.

Trump is not the last chance for national populism in America. He is just the beginning. He was not the last chance for white America. He was the system's last chance to preserve itself in the face of massive demographic change. When Trump is no longer President, our mantra must be "Trumpism has not failed. Trumpism has never been tried." Only then we will start calling it national populism, and if we play the long game, we will have created a whole new political movement to secure its triumph.

The bad news is that Trump turned out to be better at campaigning than governing. The good news is that he will soon go back on the campaign trail, and if "Send her back" is any indication, it is going to be another magnificent opportunity to move the national mind in our direction. When that time comes, I hope our best propagandists will not sit it out, sulking in their tents.

If we are going to effectively advance our ideas, we cannot get distracted by the politics of personality, including our own personal issues. We must never lose sight of our ultimate aim, which is a homeland for whites in North America.

Counter-Currents, July 22, 2019

The UK Voted for National Populism

When Brexit won and I heard "Land of Hope and Glory" played at one of the celebrations, I found myself tearing up, much to my surprise. Of course, it makes sense. England is my ancestral homeland. But actually *feeling* it came as a surprise. It was one of those "welcome to the human race" experiences.

I was similarly delighted with the outcome of the 2019 UK general election, which was good for national populism and ethnonationalism not just in Great Britain but around the world.

White nations want national populism: sensible social conservatism + a state that is willing to intervene in the economy to protect the working and middle classes from plutocracy and globalization. The cosmopolitan elites that rule us want just the opposite: social liberalism + globalization and oligarchy.

Thus our ruling elites have made an art of not giving the voters what they want. In 2016, the UK voted for Brexit, and the political establishment has done everything in its power not to deliver it. In 2016, the American people voted for national populism and elected Donald Trump, but the political establishment simply dug in its heels against Trump's national populist agenda, although they did allow him to deliver tax cuts to billionaires, pardons to Jewish criminals, and basically anything Benjamin Netanyahu asked for.

Now Boris Johnson has won a crushing victory over the Left by promising to "Get Brexit Done." The Conservative Party gained 48 seats for a solid majority, whereas Labour lost 60 seats. Now Johnson must assert the will of the people over the UK establishment.

There is really no question that the UK voted for national populism.

Boris Johnson's main election slogan was "Get Brexit Done." Beyond that, Johnson promised more funding for the National Health Service, which benefits working-class and middle-class voters. He also promised to spend more money on the North of England, which has been blighted by globalization.

This was a clear attempt to woo Labour voters, and it succeeded. In effect, Johnson offered the UK popular Labour policies + social conservatism + Brexit = national populism, whereas Labour offered popular Labour policies + social liberalism + a second referendum on Brexit (and presumably as many more referendums as necessary for the peasants to finally vote for what the elites want).

The result was the biggest defeat for Labour in decades, including the loss of seats in 24 long-time Labour strongholds.

Jeremy Corbyn made many mistakes, but I fundamentally respect his rejection of Tony Blair's New Labour, which through its embrace of neoliberalism and globalization became the party of rainbow oligarchy. Genuine Leftists like Corbyn should never be given power, but the far Left, like the labor movement, needs to exist, because capitalists can only be persuaded to be good citizens if the threat of communism haunts them every minute of their lives.

The 2019 UK general election was, in effect, the second Brexit referendum that the globalists have been whining about for more than three years, and they are not taking yet another defeat very well. Let's hope their spirits will break soon. (Perhaps Johnson's NHS should offer euthanasia to the "literally trembling" crowd on Twitter.)

The Conservatives were not the only winners of national populist votes, for the Scottish National Party also picked up 13 seats, at the expense of both Labour and the

Conservatives. When faced with a choice between populist social policies + Scottish independence or populist social policies without Scottish independence, many Scottish voters naturally chose the national populist option.

The Scottish National Party now holds 48 of Scotland's 59 seats in Parliament. Party leader Nicola Sturgeon correctly interprets this as a mandate. The SNP wants to remain in the EU, and if Johnson goes through with Brexit, Sturgeon wants another referendum on Scottish independence.

I hope she gets her way, and I would like to make a suggestion that will ensure that Scottish independence will sail through: *Let all UK voters vote on it.* Large numbers of Englishmen would jump at the chance to hand Scotland her freedom. (The same is true of Quebec independence. Western Canada would overwhelmingly support it.)

Frankly, I think the Tories are stupid to oppose Scottish independence. Scottish voters oppose the Tories not just on Brexit but on virtually every other matter of policy. The Tories would actually be stronger if Scotland became independent. (See my essays on Scottish independence.[1])

But the Tories are not alone in this bloody-minded stupidity. Right-wing Spaniards oppose Catalonian independence, even though Catalonia is a Leftist stronghold, and its departure would strengthen the Right in the rest of Spain. Likewise, countless American Republicans have a knee-jerk opposition to Calexit, even though a Calexit would enable Republican hegemony in the rest of America. (See my essay on Calexit.[2])

---

[1] Greg Johnson, "Why I Support Scottish Independence" and "'Let's Call the Whole Thing Off': In Defense of 'Petty' Nationalism," *Truth, Justice & a Nice White Country.*

[2] Greg Johnson, "In Praise of Calexit," *In Defense of Prejudice.*

Northern Ireland also wishes to remain in the EU. So if Brexit goes through, the United Kingdom may consist only of England and Wales. So be it.

As an ethnonationalist, I support the right of all European peoples to their own sovereign homelands. Different peoples, even closely related ones, *really are different*. Thus they are more likely to come into conflict if they have to live in the same system. If England and Wales want to leave the EU and Scotland and Northern Ireland don't, then they really aren't a United Kingdom, are they? The only way for all parties to get their way is to disunite the UK.

If Brexit is a good thing because of national sovereignty, then so is Scottish independence, and so is Northern Irish independence as well.

A common objection to secession movements in our circles is that Brexit or Scottish independence won't really change immigration. But if immigration will happen with or without Brexit, then it is not really a relevant issue in the first place.

Brexit will, however, allow the British to set their own immigration policies rather than Brussels. Scottish independence will allow the Scots to set their own policies rather than London. Under such circumstances, the policies they choose may not suit you, but they are more likely to suit the UK or Scotland.

The root objection to secession is that some people disapprove of the policies that free peoples might adopt. But unless you are British or Scottish or Catalonian, you are missing the whole point of national sovereignty, which is that it allows people to act in ways that others might disapprove of. That's really the whole point.

White freedom and self-determination will happen one white nation at a time. Thus White Nationalists should applaud Brexit and Scottish independence because they uphold the ethnonationalist principle and demonstrate that national sovereignty can be attained without violence. We want as many such precedents as possible.

The British people have spoken, yet again. But Boris Johnson's battle has just begun. Now he has to keep his promises in the teeth of the globalist establishment that opposes him. Nationalists of all nations wish him well.

Politics, as they say, is the art of the possible. There is no better proof that something is possible than an example of it being actual. When Brexit passed, suddenly it became conceivable in the minds of millions that Trump could be elected. And surely that change of sentiment actually helped him get elected.

Boris Johnson's victory now makes Donald Trump's re-election seem possible, and that makes it more likely. But only if Trump and the Republicans learn the right lesson: national populism is the wave of the future.[3] Unfortunately, they're not called the stupid party for nothing.

Counter-Currents, December 18, 2019

---

[3] Gregory Hood, "What the British Elections Mean for Whites," *American Renaissance*, December 17, 2019.

THE GROUPIE QUESTION IN WHITE NATIONALISM

I received this question from a *Counter-Currents* reader:

> Andrew Marantz's *Antisocial* tells the story of "Samantha," who got involved with Identity Evropa and the Alt Right, rose through the ranks, became disaffected, and then left the movement and talked to the enemy. In view of Samantha and other doxings by ex-scene groupies like Katie McHugh, should the movement simply ban women?

The short answer is: No.

First, what does it even mean to ban women from a largely anonymous online movement, which lacks any barriers to entry or standards of membership? We can't ban women from the internet. We can't ban women from reading our websites, listening to our podcasts, watching our videos, etc. We can't ban women from writing for our websites, commenting on our websites, or donating to them if they simply use pen names. (For all I know, the person who sent in the question is a woman.)

Of course some *parts* of the movement can exclude women. I don't think we should accept the essentially feminist assumption that all organizations and realms of society should admit women, much less aim for male/female parity. I also think that it is quite natural for radical politics to attract more men than women. And just as combat units and police forces function better without women, so might some White Nationalist political organizations.

But even if it were possible to *entirely* exclude women

from White Nationalist politics, doing so would be dumb and self-defeating. If women want to contribute their money, ideas, time, and social capital to the movement, that makes us stronger, not weaker. Beyond that, we are never going to actually win unless we can convince a substantial percentage of the female population that we represent their real interests. And we will never do that if we allow the tone of the movement to be set by embittered misogynists, to say nothing of people who proclaim "White Sharia" and "Islam is Right About Women."

Leftists love to dismiss realism about racial differences as racial hatred. But that's not necessarily true. Feminists love to dismiss realism about sexual differences as misogyny, the hatred of women. But that's not necessarily true either.

However, just as there really are people in our movement who hate other races, there are people in our movement who genuinely hate women.

Just as the goal of our movement should be to drain the swamp of diversity in which race-hate breeds, we should also try to address the underlying causes of hatred between the sexes.

And just as we will not achieve our goal in the racial sphere if we allow simple race hatred to define our movement, we will not achieve our goals in the sexual sphere by allowing misogynists to set the tone either.

White Nationalists are mature enough to recognize that hatred between the races and sexes is the inevitable product of the current system. We also need to be mature enough to recognize that indulging embittered haters will destroy any chance to rectify our problems.

Second, talking about excluding all women because of doxers like Katie McHugh makes no sense. Should the movement also exclude all men, because some men are doxers as well? That would put an end to 100% of doxings, but it would also put an end to the movement itself. Surely we can be a bit more surgical about excluding certain types of people to minimize such problems in the future.

Third, the very same people who want to blame women for problems in the movement also often deny that women have moral agency. But if women have no agency, then they bear no responsibility either. But clearly *somebody* is to blame for these operational security and public relations disasters, and by their own logic, misogynists would have to blame men.

And in truth, men bear a lot of the blame. By all accounts, McHugh, Samantha, and another unnamed woman who doxed Coach Finstock were not ordinary women. They were Alt Right scene groupies. Like rock groupies, they were attracted to an overwhelmingly misogynistic subculture. Women who are drawn to such environments are surely high in masochism and low in self-worth. They then worked their way through the scene, passing over nice guys until they ended up with manipulative sociopaths. But when they realized that masochistic self-indulgence was not making them happy, they bailed out.

Then, once they had become sufficiently embittered to feel justified in harming innocent people, they went to the enemy and started doxing people, including people who had only been kind to them. This is the sort of pure evil that makes people dream of the eternal fires of hell to restore justice to the world.

What makes such evil possible? I think a good part of it can be explained by bitterness. Bitterness takes root when someone is wronged and does not receive justice. Bitterness turns into a kind of neurosis. Embittered people vent their wrath not on the people who wronged them, but on innocent people who *merely remind them of the guilty parties*. And if such people have any pangs of conscience, bitterness easily silences them: "Why should I care about these people's suffering? Where were they when I was suffering? Who cared about me?"

So how do we lessen the likelihood of such disasters in the future?

First, we really need to dispel the atmosphere of misogyny in the movement, which attracts damaged people of both sexes. Race realism: yes. Race hate: no. Sex realism: yes. Hatred between the sexes: no. Our movement will never win unless we treat such hatreds as social problems to be solved. And we cannot credibly promise to solve them in society as a whole if we allow them to run rampant in our own ranks.

Second, we need to exclude groupies. But we also need to exclude the kinds of sociopathic males they gravitate toward. If we stand for the restoration of Western civilization, then we stand for monogamy, not polygamy. We stand for fidelity, not adultery. We stand for healthy relationships, not pathological ones. Which means that playboys, sluts, adulterers, and abusers are part of the problem, not part of the solution.

If someone you know is playing the field, using and discarding movement groupies, he is playing with fire. He is putting his own short-term gratification ahead of the health of our cause. That's a problem, and you need to say something.

Third, we need to drain the swamp where bitterness and wrath breed. We have to *do something* when people in our movement wrong one another. We need to have some sympathy for victims of injustice, even for victims who are not entirely innocent. And the best form of sympathy is to *give them justice*, which means there have to be punishments for wrongdoers. People who dox others are evil and deserve no sympathy today. But if they had received sympathy and justice when they were wronged, things may have worked out differently, and we would all be better off.

The Alt Right in America crashed and burned because it was run by a mafia of drunkards, druggies, sociopaths, and buffoons, as well as swarms of remora-like fanboys, sycophants, and enablers. I fear that we are going to be hearing a lot more such stories from Samantha and people like her for years to come. But the movement for white survival will not falter as long as we treat such disasters as opportunities to learn rather than excuses to quit.

Counter-Currents, October 25, 2019

Our Votes Don't Matter, But Our Ideas Do

How should White Nationalists take part in American electoral politics?

In the long run, we want our ideas to be hegemonic, the common sense of the whole political system, upheld by all the political parties.[1] We want white interests to be as sacrosanct as anti-racism, diversity, and globalization are to the major parties today. When all parties work to secure our interests, it doesn't matter who wins elections, because whites can't lose.

In the nearer term, we would like to see our ideas championed as the platform of a major political party that can actually win elections. Realistically, in the American context, that means replacing the Republican Party with a national populist party, or replacing the leadership of the Republicans with national populists.

In the still nearer term, I would like White Nationalists to become a voting bloc that is large and powerful enough to swing elections, so that politicians will actively court us and fear to cross us.

So how do we get there from here?

But maybe we're already there. After all, aren't some elections close enough for our votes to decide them? And don't we already constitute a voting bloc?

That would depend on whether enough of our people to swing an election are voters in close districts. Do we know the answer to that question? Because if we don't, then I don't think we're a voting bloc just yet, because we lack at least two important features of voting blocs: we don't know who we are—and neither do the major parties.

---

[1] See Greg Johnson, "Hegemony," *New Right vs. Old Right*.

A voting bloc is not just a set of people with shared political preferences. Such a group also has to be *visible*—visible *to themselves*, i.e., *self-conscious*, and visible *to the society around them*. White Nationalists definitely exist. White Nationalists definitely vote. But we don't know how many of us there are, where we are, and how committed we are. We don't have political organizations to gather such information or political leaders to muster the White Nationalist vote.

But if we don't know who we are and what we can do, then the political parties don't know it either, which means our votes don't figure into their electoral calculations. We simply don't matter.

But let's say we were a real voting bloc. That still doesn't give us power if we are so widely despised by the rest of the electorate that *politicians can gain more votes by snubbing us than by courting us.*

White Nationalists like to kid ourselves that we "memed Donald Trump into the White House." But is that true? Isn't it possible that the Alt Right cost Trump Republican votes and raised Democratic turnouts? Maybe. Maybe not. But until we can answer questions like that, we're not really a serious voting bloc.

So if White Nationalists aren't quite ready for politics, how do we prepare ourselves?

We must identify the necessary conditions for becoming a political force. Then we must assemble those conditions, to the best of our ability. We must begin with things that we can do right now, and we must prepare ourselves to do harder things in the future.

Let's begin with the obvious. If White Nationalism is going to be a political force, *we need more White Nationalists*.

But even if we dramatically increase the numbers of White Nationalists, we will not gain power if we are opposed by even greater numbers. Therefore, in addition to greater numbers on our side, we need *less opposition from our opponents*, for instance by sowing division among them, by converting enemies into neutral parties, and by converting neutral parties into sympathizers who will uphold the legitimacy of our participation in politics.

We are closer to victory if we get more people fighting for us and fewer people fighting against us.

How do we achieve these two goals?

We need to change people's minds. We need to convert enemies to neutrals, neutrals to sympathizers, and sympathizers to committed White Nationalists.

To change people's minds, we need to *know* their minds. We need to understand the ideas and values of people who are *already* White Nationalists, and the ideas and values of people who *might be converted* to White Nationalism. Then we need to map out how to bring the latter into our camp. We also need to understand the ideas and values of our enemies if we are to decrease their opposition to us. Armed with such knowledge, we could launch educational campaigns that would move us closer to our goals.

One could argue, of course, that we have been doing a pretty good job without such knowledge. Based simply on introspection and personal experience, a lot of us have become quite skilled at converting people. Furthermore, the rising traffic of various movement websites can be taken as testament to this success.

But how much of this rising traffic is due to our outreach, and how much of it is due simply to the problems endemic to multiculturalism and globalization? How much is rising white ethnocentrism due to our persuasive pull, as opposed to the system's dystopian push? That is another question that we really need to answer if we are to become serious contenders for power.

To do a serious study of the public mind, we need to create an institution, staff it with people with the necessary skills, and fund their studies.

We also need some sort of institute to craft White Nationalist positions on public policy issues.

Finally, we need a third institution, a political advocacy group that takes the first two groups' findings and uses them to weld White Nationalists into a self-conscious voting bloc, while laying the foundations for longer-term aims like taking over or founding a political party and eventually establishing hegemony over the entire political system.

There is a word for formulating ideas and creating institutions necessary for the pursuit of political power. We call it "metapolitics."

There's another word for pursuing political power without taking care of the metapolitical conditions. We call it LARPing, meaning "live action role playing." It is play acting.

When White Nationalists on Twitter declare, "We must punish Trump for betraying us" or take positions amounting to, "In order to punish the imaginary fascist Trump, I will deliver the presidency to an actual Jewish communist, Sanders," they are living in a fantasy world. Individually and as a group, we don't have the power to do any of those things.

In a democratic election, it seldom matters one way or another how a given individual votes, or if he votes at all. After all, when was the last time that an important election was decided by one vote?

Furthermore, as I argued above, White Nationalists have absolutely no idea if we could constitute a real swing vote in close races. And if we don't know that, politicians can hardly be faulted for ignoring us. Beyond that, we are so widely despised, most politicians would calculate that they could gain more votes by spurning us rather than catering to us.

Some people think that we can gain real power by engaging in grandiose empty talk, because of the manosphere axiom "Fake it 'til you make it." But that only works when hitting on drunken bimbos. We gain real power by assembling the real conditions of power.

Furthermore, empty talk actually undermines the pursuit of power, because it makes us look foolish, when currently the only real advantages we have in politics are speaking the truth about taboo subjects—multiculturalism, race, globalization, etc.—often in the face of overwhelming opposition, and the credibility we gain from doing that. We shouldn't be so hasty to throw such advantages away.

Before White Nationalists constitute a real political force, we need to focus on metapolitics: creating institutions and communicating ideas. Thus we need to view electoral politics as a metapolitical opportunity. Our votes don't really matter, but our ideas matter a great deal.

The eyes of the world will be fixed on the 2020 US Presidential election. In 2015, Donald Trump shattered the political establishment's agreement never to compete on multiculturalism, immigration, globalization, and anything that touches on white identity politics, lest uncontrollable populist forces be unleashed. In 2020, the establishment hopes it can defeat those forces by defeating Donald Trump. The 2020 election really will be a turning point for the USA.

The Left will make the election into a referendum on multiculturalism, race, immigration, and whether America has a future as a white nation. The mainstream Right will, as usual, surrender on all matters of principle. Trump will bluster, fudge, and flounder. White Nationalists—and the broader Dissident Right—will be the only articulate and consistent intellectual champions of nationalism, populism, and the legitimacy of white ethnic interests. These are arguments we can't lose.

No matter what the outcome of the election, we can emerge as the champions of the more than 60 million mostly white people who voted for Trump in 2016 and may show up again in 2020. Thus we should comport ourselves accordingly.

It is fortunate that the 2020 election is a golden opportunity for presenting our ideas, since it is all we really can do right now. If we want our votes to matter someday, we need to start building the institutions necessary to turn truth into power.

Counter-Currents, January 23, 2020

INDEX

Numbers in bold refer to a whole chapter or section devoted to a particular topic.

2016 United States presidential election, 43, 50, 58, 61, 63, 70, 75, 81, 107, 151–52, 208; 164–65, 193, 197, 204
2018 United States midterm elections, 1, **42–45**, 47
2019 United Kingdom general election, **193–97**
2020 United States presidential election, 2, 10, 51, 53, 58–59, 61–69, **70–75**, 79, 81, 85, 86–89, 197; aftermath of, 91–94, **95–99**, **100–109**, 207–208
4chan, 53
9/11, 57

A

academia, 50, 150
accelerationism, **161–65**
Acosta, Rene Alexander, 166–67
Adelson, Sheldon, 59
Afghanistan, 56–58
Alt Right, 83, 129, 144–47, 151, 160, 191, 198, 200–201, 204

America, see: United States
America First, 8, 15, 42, 46, 58–59, 61, 70, 164, 182; see also: United States
American exceptionalism, 59; see also: United States
American nationalism, 65–69; see also: United States
amnesty, **39–41**, 96–97
antifa, 34, 36–37, 39, 45, 96, 99, 103, 108, 110, 111, 123, 125, 128, 131, 137–38, 141, 146, 152, 155
anti-racism, 9, 14, 18–19, 22, 53, 83, 203
Arbery, Ahmaud, 24, 28, 31
Aristotle, 184
Asians, 53–54, 81, 88, 98, 102
assimilation, 187
Austrian economics, 52

B

ballot fraud; see electoral fraud
banana republics, 64, **91–94**, 169
Biden, Joe, 1–2, 39, 72–75,

83, 85, 86–87, 89, 91–
93, 95–98, 103–106
Big Tech, 92, 105
bitterness, 200–201
Black Lives Matter, 2–3,
18–22, 23–30, 31–34,
36–37, 39, 96, 99, 100
blacks, 19–22, 23–28, 30,
34, 35, 37–38, 39–40,
73, 75, 77–79, 81, 82,
88, 98, 102; criminality
of, 2–3, 20–22, **23–30**,
31–34, 35, 37, 41, 78,
178, 189
Blair, Tony, 194
Bloomberg, Mike, 72–73,
166
Bowden, Jonathan, 40
Bowers, Robert, 149, 155
Breivik, Anders Behring,
111–14, 117, 123, 132, 136,
144–48
Brexit, 157, **193–97**
Brown, Michael, 18–19, 24,
28, 31
Bush, George W., 56–57
Buttigieg, Pete, 72–73

C

Calexit, 195
California, 87; Calexit,
195–96
Camp of the Saints, The
(Raspail), 43
Capitalism, 13, 48, 75
Cargo cults, 88
Carlson, Tucker, 20, 101
Catalonia, 195–96

Cato Institute, 75
censorship, 19, 55, 79, 84–
89, 96, 104–105, 151–54,
158
Charlottesville (Unite the
Right), 65, 68
Chauvin, Derek, 4, 30, 31–
34, 35–38
China, 8, 10, 13–14, 57
civic nationalism, 62, 101,
187, 192
civil disobedience, 108
Civil War (American), 40,
67
civilization, 3, 30, 37, 201;
American, 49; Western, 201
Clinton, Bill, 166, 173
Clinton, Hillary, 14, 58, 61,
64, 86, 164
colonialism, 30, 40
common good, 5, 8–9, 13–
14, 16, 71, 88, 175, 187
communism or communists, 38, 77–78,
110–11, 115, 124, 137, 178,
194, 206
conservatism, 10–12, 38,
48, 51, 61, 65, 67, 81,
97, 151, 185–86, 193–94
Conservative Party (UK),
193, 195
conspiracy theories, 14, 67,
97, 170–75, 178, 180–81
Constitution (United
States), 87, 94, 172
Copenhagen, 110, 115, 137–
38

Corbyn, Jeremy, 194
coronavirus, see: COVID-19
Cortés, Juan Donoso, 77
Costello, Jef, 18
Counter-Currents, 88, 89, 99, 124, 136
COVID-19, **5–12**, **13–17**, 29, 32, 92, 96
crime (black), 2–3, 20–22, 23–30, 31–34, 35, 37, 41, 78, 178, 189

D
Dabney, Robert Lewis, 185
De Blasio, Bill, 174
deep state, 7–8, 100, 109, 164
democracy, 7, 12, 49, 63–64, 71, 77, 87, 92–93, 108, 124, 139, 151, 171–72, 206; Nordic Social Democracy, 124, 139
Democratic Party, 11, 15, 42–43, 46–48, 51, 54, 59, 61–64, 80, 96–97, 99, 100, 108, 138, 164, 173; and the 2020 presidential election, 70–75, 84, 89, 91–94, 107, 204
Denmark, 110, 138–39
deplatforming, 55, 58, 87, 105, 136, 151–53
Dershowitz, Alan, 166
discrimination, 99, 100, 102, 172
diversity, 4, 9–10, 12, 50, 55, 67, 104, 150, 187–88, 199, 203
Dutton, Edward, 111, 122

E
Eatwell, Roger, 54–55, 104, 156–57
economic nationalism, 46
economics, 6, 9, 28, 51–52, 193
economy (United States), 2–3, 10–11, 13–16, 42, 47, 70, 77, 96, 161–62; of the world, 55, 104, 153
egalitarianism, 5, 110, 186
electoral fraud, 2, 50, 62–64, 71–74, 89, 92, 94–95, 104, 107
elitism, 3, 48
Elizabeth II, Queen of England, 166
Epstein, Jeffrey, 125, 134, **166–76**
ethnocentrism, 30, 205
ethnonationalism, 77–78, 96, 193, 196–97
European Union, 6
evangelical Christians, 81

F
Facebook, 92, 105, 172
FBI (US Federal Bureau of Investigation), 20–21, 27, 166, 173
feminism, 198–99
Ferguson Effect, 23
Filter Nyheter, 111, 114–16, 123, 146–47
First Amendment, 43, 64,

79, 84–85, 95–97, 104, 172; see also: freedom of speech; censorship
Floyd, George, 18–19, 24, 26, 28–29, **31–34**, 35
Fredericksen, Mette, 138–39
"free market" ideology, 10, 51–52
free trade, 8, 164
freedom of speech, 104–105, 117, 119, 130–32, 134, 138, 141, 148, 149, 153, 163, 172; see also: First Amendment; censorship
Freemasonry, 67
Frey, Jacob, 36
Fuentes, Nick, 59

G
Gab, 53
GDP, 16
gerrymandering, 63
Giraldi, Philip, 167
Giuliani, Rudolph, 173
globalism and globalists, 3, 6–7, 12, 48, 75, 97, 131, 197
globalization, 1, 50, 55, 61, 70, 81, 98, 104–105, 109, 138, 150, 153, 157, 193–94, 203, 205, 207
Goethe, Johann Wolfgang von, 184
Goodwin, Matthew, 54–55, 104, 156–57
GOP, see: Republican Party
Great Replacement, 85, 86, 92, 106, 173

H
Harris, Kamala, 66, 86–87, 89
hegemony, 203, 206
Hispanics, 81, 88, 98
history, 40–41, 63, 76–77, 165, 171, 185
Hofstadter, Richard, 177–78
Holocaust, 40, 67
Hopkins, Katie, 59
Houck, Richard, 21
human biodiversity, 110–11, 122, 147

I
Identitarian Movement, (Austria), 152
identitarianism and identitarians, 87, 100, 103, 118, 129, 145–47, 152
identity politics, 51, 67, 70–71, 81–82, 98–99, **100–101**, 106
immigration (United States), 6, 43, 47, 50–51, 61–64, 70–71, 81, 92–93, 98, 163–64, 182, 189, 191, 207; into white countries, 55, 104, 112, 117, 138–39, 157, 177, 187, 196
individualism, 5–6, 8–9, 13
Insurrection Act, 34

IQ, 23, 26, 73, 81, 168
Iran, **56–60**
Iraq, 57–59
irony, 116, 160
Islam, 199; see also: Islamophobia, Muslims
Islamophobia, 139
Israel, 14–15, 56, 59, 60, 167–68

J
January 6, 2021, protests, 4, 107–108
Jews, 43, 47, 59, 60, 62, 63, 78, 81, 82, 88, 98, 144, 166–67, 193, 206
Johnson, Boris, 193–94, 197
journalism and journalists, 19, 103, 129, 135, 141, 171, 174, 176
justice, 3, 4, 24, 31, 33–34, 36–38, 103, 159, 200–201

K
Kissinger, Henry, 166
Klobuchar, Amy, 72–73
Koch brothers, 75

L
Labour Party, 193–95
LARPing, 206
law enforcement, 22; see also: police
liberalism, 6, 8–9, 12, 13, 26, 30, 38, 59, 77–78, 149, 187–88, 193–94; classical, 5, 10, 13–14

libertarianism, 10, 75
liberty, 187

M
MacDonald, Heather, 23
MacDonald, Kevin, 86, 110, 122
Maddow, Rachel, 106
mainstream media, 11, 34, 50, 100, 115, 121, 135, 138, 169; see also: journalists
Martin, Trayvon, 18–19, 24, 28, 31
Marxism, 71
Maxwell, Ghislaine, 167
Maxwell, Robert, 167
McCain, John, 163–64
McCarthy, Joseph, 178
McHugh, Katie, 198–200
memes, 50–51, 53, 83, 151, 190
metapolitics, 13, 45, 75, 83, 99, 110, 139, 151–52, 154, 159–60, 206–207
Mexico, 63; see also: Hispanics
Midjord, Fróði, 110, 114, 119, 122, 141
Midwest, 81
middle class, 48, 55, 157, 193–94
Minneapolis, 34, 36
Minnesota, 34
miscegenation, 187
misogyny, 199–200
morality, 8–11, 39–40, 45, 78, 82–84, 88, 99, 101–

102, 103–104, 111, 139, 149–51, 157, 158, 186–87
multiculturalism, 1, 9–10, 13, 38, 45, 55, 76, 104–105, 117–18, 122, 133, 139, 150, 153, 157, 177, 187, 189, 205, 207
Muslims, 46, 57, 60, 120, 131, 153, 189; see also: Islam; Islamophobia

N

narcissism, 180–81, 182
nationalism, 3, 10, 12, 42, 48, 66, 97–98, 105, 139, 197; see also: American nationalism; civic nationalism; economic nationalism; ethnonationalism; white nationalism
national populism, 54–55, 59, 146, **156–57**, 186–87, 203; and COVID-19, 13–16; and Trump, 44, 50–51, 61, 64–66, 68–69, 79, 87, 104–105, 151, 191–92, 193, 197; and the UK, **193–97**; see also: populism
National Populism: The Revolt Against Liberal Democracy (Eatwell and Goodwin), 54–55, 104, 156–57
National Socialism, 139
naturalization, 187
neo-Nazism, 68, 113, 151

neoconservatism, 56, 58–59
neoliberalism, 71, 97
New York City, 169, 173–74
Norway, Greg Johnson's expulsion from, **110–20, 121–40, 141–48**
Nyborg, Helmuth, 111, 122

O

Obama, Barack, 27, 42, 162–64
Omar, Ilhan, 189
open borders, 9, 13, 85, 96–97, 109, 131
opioid crisis, 50
O'Rourke, Beto, 63
Oslo, see: Norway

P

paranoia, 155, 177–80
Parler, 105
paternalism, 26, 29–30
patriotism, 1, 67, 81, 108
Pelosi, Nancy, 1
Pizzagate, 173
polarization, 1, 55, 57, 77, 79, 97
police: American, 3, 18–22, 23, 27–29, 30, 31–33, 35–37; Norwegian, 115–16, 118, 123–24, 127, 132–34, 136–38, **141–48**
populism, 14, 43–44, 47–48, 66, 70, 81, 85, 97–98, 107, 109, 169, 175, 207; national (see: national populism)

protectionism, 13, 46, 48, 81, 157, 164
psychology, 28–29, 81, 83, 162

Q
QAnon, 101, 108, 173
Qtards, 89
Quinn, Spencer, 86

R
race realism, 101–102, 199, 201
racial separation, 27, 30, 34, 38, 76–79, 149
racism, 9–11, 14, 22, 23, 31, 35, 38, 54, 78, 82–84, 88, 90, 91, 99, 100, 102, 187, 189–90; see also: anti-racism
Republican Party, 11, 13–16, 42–44, 56, 59, 81–84, 87, 91–92, 96–97, 99, 101, 195, 203; and Trump, 11, 43, 46–48, 58, 61, 63–66, 70–71, 89, 100, 105, 107–109, 164, 191, 197
Rhodesia, 162
riots, 2–3, 23, 31, 39, 77–78, 96, 99, 108, 152
Robinson, Tommy, 59
Rome, 76
Romney, Mitt, 162–64
Roof, Dylann, 149
Russia, 57, 171

S
Sailer strategy, 82
Salman, King of Saudi Arabia, 166
Sanders, Bernie, 71–75, 206
Scandza Forum, 110, 114–16, 118, 121–23, 128, 130, 134, 137, 141, 144–45, 148; see also: Norway
Schengen Zone, 6, 131
Schmitt, Carl, 77
Scottish National Party, 194–95
Second Amendment, 64, 87, 95–97
self-defense, 19, 38, 114n5, 158–59
Shamir, Yitzhak, 167
slavery, 40
Smollet, Jussie, 31
Social Credit economics, 51
Social Democrats (Denmark), 138
social media, 4, 18–19, 151
social trust, 10, 16, 156, 162, 169, 172, 175
Soleimani, Qasem, 56–58
South Africa, 162
Southern nationalism, 67
Spencer, Richard, 83–84, 87, 189–90
Steyer, Tom, 72–73
Sturgeon, Nicola, 195
Sun Tzu, 160
Syria, 47

T
Taliban, 56
Tarrant, Brenton, 149, 153–

55, 158–160, 163
Taylor, Jared, 86
Tech giants, see: Big Tech
technology, 52
terrorism, domestic, 103, 106, 173; foreign, 57–58; Left-wing, 36–37; Right-wing, 111–13, 114n5, 116–17, 123–24, 128, 144, 146–48, **149–60**, 163
Third World, 47, 62, 131
time preferences, 28, 65, 81, 188
Trump, Donald: and 2016 United States presidential election, 43, 50, 58, 61, 63, 70, 75, 81, 107, 151–52, 208; 164–65, 193, 197, 204; and 2018 United States midterm elections, **42–45**, 47; and 2020 United States presidential election, 2, 10, 51, 53, 58–59, 61–69, **70–75**, 79, 81, 85, 86–89, 197; and aftermath of 2020 election, 91–94, **95–99, 100–109**, 207–208; accomplishments of, 48–49, 86, 95, 98, 106; and antifa, 34, 96; response to COVID-19, 11, 14–15; and Jeffrey Epstein, 166, 173; faults of, 47, 50, 51, 54, 56–58, 62–63, 98–99, 100, 105, 182, 192; foreign policy of, 56–59, 181–82 (see also: America First); and the Republican Party, 11, 43, 46–48, 58, 61, 63–66, 70–71, 89, 100, 105, 107–109, 164, 191, 197; supporters of, 48, 94, 96, 98, 103, 106, 108–109, 151, 189; and White Nationalism, see: White Nationalism
Trump Derangement Syndrome, 8
Twitter, 65, 92, 105, 194, 206

U

United Kingdom, **193–97**
United States, 2016 United States presidential election, 43, 50, 58, 61, 63, 70, 75, 81, 107, 151–52, 208; 164–65, 193, 197, 204; 2018 United States midterm elections, **42–45**, 47; 2020 United States presidential election, 2, 10, 51, 53, 58–59, 61–69, **70–75**, 79, 81, 85, 86–89, 197; aftermath of 2020 election, 91–94, **95–99, 100–109**, 207–208; blacks in, 19–22, 23–28, 30, 34, 35, 37–

38, 39–40, 73, 75, 77–79, 81, 82, 88, 98, 102; conservatism in, 10, 13–14, 186; Constitution, 87, 94, 172; COVID-19, 7–9, 14–15, 17; downfall of, 1–3, 53, 62, 70, 77–78, 85, 91–94; foreign policy of, 56–60; immigration into, 6, 43, 47, 50–51, 61–64, 70–71, 81, 92–93, 98, 163–64, 182, 189, 191, 207; ruling class of, 8, 18, 21, 48, 109, 166, 193; people of, 15, 20, 34, 37, 49–50, 64–65, 74, 89, 93, 99, 100–102, 109, 169, 191–92, 193; see also: America First; American exceptionalism; American nationalism
universal basic income, 51–53
universalism, 186–87

V

voter fraud, 50, 62, 92, 95; see also: electoral fraud
voter identification, 91–92, 94

W

Wallace, Bubba, 31
Warren, Elizabeth, 60, 66, 72, 74
White Nationalism, 1, 30, 54–55, 95–96, 203–208; and accelerationism, **161–63**; and American nationalism, 67–69; paranoia in, **177–82**; and terrorism, 147, **149–60**; and Trump, 44–45, 46–50, 58, 63–66, 70, 75, 81, 84–85, 98, 189–91, 204–208; and the UK, 197; and Andrew Yang, 51, 53–54
White Nationalist Manifesto, The (Johnson), 4, 54, 156, 177n1
white privilege, 102, 110–11, 117, 121–23, 128, 147, 171
white supremacy, 102, 121, 135
wignats (wigger nationalists), **61–69**, **81–85**
women, 198–200
women's suffrage, 185
working class, 48, 55, 81, 157, 193–94

X

xenophobia, 9, 10, 13, 177

Y

Yang, Andrew, **46–55**
YouTube, 65, 105, 173, 198

Z

Zimmerman, George, 19

ABOUT THE AUTHOR

GREG JOHNSON, Ph.D., is Editor-in-Chief of Counter-Currents Publishing Ltd. and the *Counter-Currents* webzine.

He is the author of seventeen books, including *Confessions of a Reluctant Hater* (San Francisco: Counter-Currents, 2010; second, expanded ed., 2016); *New Right vs. Old Right* (Counter-Currents, 2013); *Truth, Justice, & a Nice White Country* (Counter-Currents, 2015); *In Defense of Prejudice* (Counter-Currents, 2017); *You Asked for It: Selected Interviews*, vol. 1 (Counter-Currents, 2017); *The White Nationalist Manifesto* (Counter-Currents, 2018; second ed., 2019); *Toward a New Nationalism* (Counter-Currents, 2019); *From Plato to Postmodernism* (Counter-Currents, 2019); *It's Okay to Be White: The Best of Greg Johnson* (Hollywood: Ministry of Truth, 2020); *Graduate School with Heidegger* (Counter-Currents, 2020); *Here's the Thing: Selected Interviews*, vol. 2 (Counter-Currents, 2020); and *White Identity Politics* (Counter-Currents, 2020).

Under the pen name Trevor Lynch, he is the author of *Trevor Lynch's White Nationalist Guide to the Movies* (Counter-Currents, 2012), *Son of Trevor Lynch's White Nationalist Guide to the Movies* (Counter-Currents, 2015); *Return of the Son of Trevor Lynch's CENSORED Guide to the Movies* (Counter-Currents, 2019); and *Trevor Lynch: Part Four of the Trilogy* (Counter-Currents, 2020).

His writings have been translated into Czech, Danish, Dutch, Estonian, French, German, Greek, Hungarian, Norwegian, Polish, Portuguese, Russian, Slovak, Spanish, Swedish, and Ukrainian.

www.ingramcontent.com/pod-product-compliance
Lightning Source LLC
Chambersburg PA
CBHW030854170426
43193CB00009BA/605